THE LITTLE BOOK

OF

ARMAGH

BARRY FLYNN

The
History
Press
Ireland

First published 2017

The History Press Ireland
50 City Quay
Dublin 2
Ireland
www.thehistorypress.ie

The History Press Ireland is a member of Publishing Ireland,
the Irish Book Publishers' Association

British Library Cataloguing in Publication Data.
A catalogue record for this book is available from the British Library.

ISBN 978 1 84588 366 9

Typesetting and origination by The History Press
Printed and bound by TJ International

CONTENTS

INTRODUCTION

ARMAGH: THE ORCHARD COUNTY OF IRELAND

It's my own Irish home
far across the foam
although I've often left it
in foreign lands to roam
no matter where I wander
through cities near or far
sure, my heart's at home in old Ireland
in the County of Armagh.

The famed song quoted above, 'The Boys from the County Armagh', begins: 'There's one fair county in Ireland, with memories so glorious and grand, where nature has lavished its bounty, it's the orchard of Erin's green land'. Armagh is an enigma. Located in the ancient province of Ulster, it the smallest of the six counties of Northern Ireland and, at 1,254 square miles, comes in at twenty-seventh in size among Ireland's thirty-two counties. It borders counties Monaghan and Louth to the south in the Irish Republic, County Down to the east, County Tyrone and Lough Neagh to the north and north-west respectively.

In historical terms, the name of the city and county was derived from 'Ard Mhacha', meaning 'Macha's height'. Macha was the ancient Irish goddess whose husband boasted that she could outrun the king of Ulster's fastest chariot. Despite being heavily pregnant, she won her race then gave birth to twins and died. In her dying pain, embarrassed at having to give birth in public, she placed a blessing and a curse on the people of Ulster, which would last for 'nine times nine generations'. Macha's name became synonymous with Armagh and is preserved also at Navan Fort, a tree ring fort that was home to the ancient rulers of Ulster. In Irish, its name is 'Emain Macha' and lies two miles west of the city and was the earliest provincial capital of Ulster. Early history tells us that, Armagh was home to the Ulidia clan and ruled over by the Red Branch, whose seat of power was also at Navan Fort. In the fourth century, the region was invaded by the Colla clan, who ruled until the twelfth century.

The landscape of the county is divided between the rich farming lands in the north and the rugged hills in the south. The highest point is the extinct volcano Slieve Gullion at 573m, where folklore is preserved and celebrated in the fabled story of Fionn McCool, who was tricked into swimming to the bottom of the mountain's lake by a beautiful young woman who claimed that she had dropped her golden ring into the bottomless pond. On finding the ring, Fionn emerged from the lake to discover that he had been tricked by a witch and had lost his youth. The summit of Slieve Gullion affords a view of nine of Ireland's counties.

The county and its people have made an impact at many levels throughout the world. In fact, it could be said that Armagh has punched well above its weight. It was the birthplace of the Orange Order in 1795. In the 1960s, the singer Tommy Makem helped to redefine Irish folk music and opened it up to a new audience throughout the world; one of his great admirers was none other than Bob Dylan. In the sporting world, a certain William McCrum from Milford invented the penalty kick in soccer and changed forever the dynamics of the world's most popular sport. Born in Armagh in 1819, Arthur Hunter Palmer emigrated to Australia in 1838, becoming the fifth Premier of Queensland in 1870. However, arguably the most famous politician to have been born in Armagh was Ian Richard Kyle Paisley in 1926. Paisley would found the Free Presbyterian Church in 1951 and end his career in politics as First Minister of Northern Ireland. In military history, Field Marshal Sir John Greer Dill was born in Lurgan in 1881. He served in the British Army during the First and Second World Wars. From May 1940 to December 1941, he was the Chief of the Imperial General Staff, the professional head of the British Army.

Armagh is particularly important for being the seat of St Patrick, who made Armagh Ireland's ecclesiastical capital and was where he established his main church. Armagh has been the spiritual capital of Ireland for 1,500 years and the seat of both Protestant and Catholic archbishops. It is also the only city in the world to contain two cathedrals named after the same saint. St Patrick's Church of Ireland Cathedral, as it is today known, was founded in AD 445. Remarkably, it has been destroyed and rebuilt seventeen times since then. It is also believed to be the burial place of the ancient Irish king, Brian Boru. The Catholic Cathedral of St Patrick was built in various phases between 1840 and 1904 in Gothic style. When the famine came to Ireland, work on the building was stopped, but the church opened eventually in 1873 thanks to fundraising and donations.

Armagh's city status was formally recognised only in 1995. The famous Georgian city contains many buildings of note. The Armagh Observatory, which opened in 1790, has long been a world leader in astronomy. In 1967, the more modern Armagh Planetarium was opened. Armagh Public Library, one of the oldest in Ireland, contains a superb collection of seventeenth- and eighteenth-century texts, including Jonathan Swift's annotated first-edition copy of his famed *Gulliver's Travels*. Armagh is celebrated as the 'Orchard County' or the 'Orchard of Ireland'. The middle of the county comes alive each year as pink flowers of apple trees come into bloom. There has been a history of apple growing in Armagh dating back 3,500 years and over 4,000 acres are dedicated to the fruit.

This book aims to bring to light the many stories that have been lost in the mists of time. Stories of ordinary people doing extraordinary things. It also hopes to provide a glimpse into the past of Armagh, the class and sectarian divisions, stories of hangings and skulduggery, personal endeavour, failure and little-known facts. It is my hope that the stories retold within this book will help to shed further light on Armagh, its people and places.

1

INDIVIDUALS AND PLACES OF NOTE IN THE ORCHARD COUNTY

A CITY OF GEORGIAN SPLENDOUR

The creation of the Georgian city of Armagh can be attributed to one Lord Rokeby, Richard Robinson, who was born in Yorkshire in 1709, and served as the Dean of Christ Church Cathedral in Dublin, before being appointed as Church of Ireland Primate in 1765. He was from a wealthy background and was determined to use his affluence and power to found and maintain charitable

and educational institutions, particularly within his adopted city of Armagh. He also wished to create a city that was fit to serve as the ecclesiastical capital of Ireland, but he was dismayed by the state of Armagh in the 1760s; it consisted largely of mud huts and thatched cottages and the cathedral was roofed with shingles. Robinson's grand plan for Armagh was supported through public subscription and generous contributions from within his own fortune.

His Grace initially employed the services of the architect Thomas Cooley, who was responsible for the design of the Royal School, the Primate's Palace and the library. When Cooley died in 1784, Francis Johnston was appointed to continue the work. Johnston remains one of Armagh's most notable sons. He was a founder of the Royal Hibernian Society and was responsible for the design of the Armagh Observatory, the county courthouse and the museum. Robinson died in Bristol in October 1794, aged 85. His body was interred in the cathedral in Armagh, where a monument was erected to his memory.

His portrait and bust were placed in the hall of Christ Church in Oxford, an institution to which he was also a generous benefactor.

THE BURIAL OF BRIAN BORU

The Battle of Clontarf took place on Good Friday, 23 April 1014, and saw the conclusion of two centuries of warfare between the Irish Celtic chieftains and the invading Norsemen, who had taken a firm foothold in Ireland. In Munster, Brian Boru had defeated the Viking armies on several occasions. His ultimate aim was to unite the Celtic kingdoms under one high king. In 1005, the king had donated 10 ounces of gold to the clergy in Armagh and decreed that the ancient city was the ecclesiastical capital of Ireland. It is estimated that between 7–10,000 men were killed in the battle, one of which was Brian Boru. It is said that Brodar, a Danish commander, retreated from the battle and his path led him directly to the hill upon which sat Brian Boru's tent. When he realised who was in the tent, he attacked it and killed Brian Boru and his old companion Conaing, who were on their knees, praying.

Prior to his death, the king had bequeathed his soul to God and willed that his body be buried in Armagh. As a funeral offering, the clergy of Armagh were provided with over 200 oxen. Boru's body was accompanied by his nephew to Swords in Dublin. The cortège made its way to Armagh through Duleek and the bones of Brian Boru are said to be buried in the North Wall of Saint Patrick's Church of Ireland Cathedral, Armagh, which dates back to medieval times. In the west wall of the north transept is a granite slab, placed there in 1914, commemorating the burial on the north side of the cathedral of Brian Boroimhe (Boru), High King of Ireland, in 1014.

'THE BARD OF ARMAGH'

The famous song, 'The Streets of Laredo', was inspired by many older songs, most famously 'The Bard of Armagh'. In that song, the bard is called 'the bold Phelim Brady', which was the name the bard went under as he tramped over the hills of South Armagh with a fiddle under his arm during times of persecution in the late 1600s. This strolling minstrel was Bishop Patrick Donnelly and it was by adopting this alter ego that the bishop was able to travel the county. Born near Cookstown, Donnelly was ordained in Armagh by Oliver Plunkett and was made a bishop in the months before the Battle of the Boyne. He served as a bishop for twenty-five years, during which he dressed in tattered clothes and visited fairs and markets, playing tunes and ministering to his flock. His 'palace' was a mud hut in Slieve Gullion. He died in 1716 and, under cover of night, he was delivered back to his native Tyrone to be buried.

THE GREAT MASTER MCGRATH

I've known many greyhounds that filled me with pride,
In the days that are gone, but it can't be denied,

That the greatest and the bravest that the world ever saw,
Was our champion of champions, great Master McGrath.

Armagh is justly proud of the achievements of the great Irish coursing champion, Master McGrath. Owned by Charles Brownlow, the 2nd Lord Lurgan, the greyhound was born in 1866 in County Waterford and was sired by Brownlow's coursing champion, Dervock. As a pup, he was considered underweight and was due to be put down, but was spared when a kennel boy named Master McGrath pleaded for the dog's life. The dog was given the name 'Master McGrath' and went on to become one of the most famous coursing greyhounds of his day, both in Ireland and England. Master McGrath was entered in England's prestigious Waterloo Cup in 1868, at just 2 years of age, and, against the odds, took the cup back to Ireland. In 1869, over 12,000 people gathered at Altcar to see Master McGrath beat the Scottish favourite, Bab-at-the-Bowster, in what many consider to be the greatest ever coursing match. The dogs were neck and neck until Master McGrath pulled ahead to achieve his second Waterloo Cup win.

With an epic third title in the offing in 1870, Lord Lurgan's greyhound lost the opportunity to win the triple crown when he fell through ice on the course while pursuing a hare and was narrowly saved from drowning. Lord Lurgan, who, along with scores of people in Lurgan, was said to have lost a fortune to the bookmakers that year, vowed that the dog would never course again. However, he relented and in 1871 the dog competed at the Waterloo Cup in Liverpool, where he was paraded before Queen Victoria, who is alleged to have fed the dog biscuits 'from her own hand'. Prior to travelling to Liverpool, it was said that Lord Lurgan had insured his greyhound for £6,000 in Belfast. In the event, Master McGrath made history when he won his third Waterloo Cup, beating his first cousin Pretender in the final. In all, Lord Lurgan won over £10,000 in prize money and retired his dog to stud after the event.

However, within a year, Master McGrath was dead. He died of heart disease which had already ended his career as a sire. During the post-mortem, it was discovered that the greyhound had an unusually large heart, twice the size of a normal dog's.

Known by the pet name 'Dicksie' and in racing circles as 'The Immortal Black', he lost only once in thirty-seven courses and is commemorated by a stained glass window in Shankill Parish Church, Main Street, Lurgan. A Master McGrath sculpture, which had been commissioned by the Brownlow family in Lurgan, was gifted to the local council and erected outside the Civic Centre in 2013.

A SAD AFFAIR AT THE PALACE DEMESNE

Home to the Church of Ireland Lord Primate of Armagh from 1770–1975, the Palace Demesne is located in an area of extensive parkland south of the centre of Armagh city. The palace was the main residence of the Church of Ireland Archbishops of Armagh and latterly the headquarters of Armagh City Council. On Monday, 15 September 1884, tragedy visited the house and Mrs Charlotte Henrietta Milner, daughter of Marcus Beresford, Archbishop of Armagh and Primate of All Ireland from 1862 until his death in 1885. Early in the afternoon of the day in question, Henry Davenport, a servant of the primate, was approached by a maid who told him that Mrs Milner was in a closet which was locked from the inside. The servant got a chair, looked through the fanlight and saw the woman hanging by a handkerchief, which had been tied to a window. Mrs Davenport, who was aged 50, had been widowed some years previously and was receiving treatment for depression from her doctor. The primate had been in poor health for a number of years and the sudden death of his daughter may have precipitated his own death in December 1885.

TAYTO CRISPS AND TANDRAGEE

One of County Armagh's most famous culinary delights is Tayto cheese-and-onion potato crisps, which are produced in Tandragee, at the famous Tandragee Castle. Established in 1956 by the Hutchinson family, the product is world-famous and is one of the tastes of home yearned for by Northern Irish expatriates living far from home. At both George Best Belfast City Airport and Belfast International Airport, the famous red-and-yellow packets are prominently displayed in the arrivals areas as they are such a unique and popular local product. It is said that within Tandragee Castle, there is a closely guarded room where the inimitable Tayto flavour is created to the same recipe that has been used for the last sixty years. Only a select few know the secret recipe, which has been passed down from generation to generation to the current day.

The original Tandragee Castle is over 500 years old and was originally the home of the O'Hanlon clan. In 1619, King James I confiscated the castle from the O'Hanlon's and the ruins of the property were given to the Duke of Manchester (of the Montagu family) in the 1800s. The present incarnation of the castle was built in 1837. Despite holding large swathes of land in County Armagh, the Montagu family was bankrupted by the gambling of its 9th Duke, William Montagu. Born on March 1877, William Montagu was educated at Eton and Trinity College, Cambridge, and succeeded his father when he was still a minor. The duke inherited a grand estate, which included lavish residences such as Tandragee Castle and Kimbolton Castle in Huntington, England.

In 1926, the family was forced to sell off much of its riches in Tandragee to cover its debts. On 6 September, a seven-day sale began at the castle which saw hundreds arrive by means of all kinds of conveyances, from Rolls Royces to donkeys, all keen to buy what they could of the opulent artefacts on offer. The castle contained a marvellous red marble entrance hall, together with an array of Turkish baths which were estimated to have cost £50,000 to install. In the castle, there were 150 rooms and the corridors were adorned with 150 yards of rich red Wilton carpet. It was reported that the building contained 'everything that art and science can suggest – libraries, pictures, furniture, carvings and a private chapel'. The auction was overseen by Mr Garnet Holt of Newry, who advised the press that there were over twenty chests of riches belonging to the family in London which could not be transported due to excessive costs.

The Montagu connection with Tandragee and Northern Ireland ended in 1955, when the 10th Duke sold the castle, which was in need of repair, to a visionary local businessman, Thomas Hutchinson. In 1956, Hutchinson saw a gap in the Ulster culinary market so he started making Tayto crisps, thus creating one of the world's best-loved brands of crisps and snacks. Tayto became one of the first companies to sell different flavours of crisps, with 'Smoky Bacon' and 'Prawn Cocktail' being two of the most popular, after the classic 'Cheese and Onion'.

A WORLD OF FOOTBALLING PAIN AND GLORY – ALL BECAUSE OF AN ARMAGH MAN!

If any player shall deliberately trip or hold an opposing player or deliberately handle the ball within twelve yards of his own goal-line, the referee shall, on appeal, award the opposing side a penalty kick, to be taken any twelve yards from the goal-line.

William McCrum's penalty proposal

As founder of the Mid-Ulster Football Association, William McCrum's contribution to the history of association football was not merely limited to administrative duties, as the following story illustrates.

The drama of penalty shoot-outs to decide soccer matches has kept many fans around the world on the edge of their seats as tournaments come to a climax. However, the 'sudden death' method was invented not in the hallowed halls of FIFA, but in William Street in Milford on an unassuming field in 1890.

William McCrum was born in 1865 and grew up in the Manor House in Milford, one of the most scientifically advanced homes in Victorian Ireland. It was one of first houses to use hydroelectricity and each of its many bathrooms was fitted with a Turkish bath. McCrum's family was affluent and William had the opportunity to become master of a range of sports. Frustrated by defenders who would trip or bring down forwards in association football, McCrum, or 'Master Willie' as he was known, felt that players and teams needed to be penalised to preserve the spirit of the game. His solution was a penalty kick, which has since entered into the psyche of the game. His ideal of a one-on-one battle of wits was introduced locally, but frowned upon by the powers that were. The English authorities were horrified at the 'Irishman's motion' or what they labelled the 'death penalty'. However, when the football authorities accepted the penalty kick (Law 13) in 1891, the game of football changed forever.

In 2001, the historic spot where William McCrum's idea was first realised was threatened by bulldozers when a planning application for sixty-four houses was proposed, a move which had locals up in arms. Although the field was used mainly for grazing, Joe McManus, chairman of the

Milford Community Development Association, declared, 'This field should be sacred ground.' McManus, a local historian in Milford, added:

> McCrum was the son of the village's founder and a goalkeeper with Milford Football Club. It was in 1890 that the talented shot-stopper dreamed up the idea. His proposal went to the Irish Football Association and then to England, where it wasn't thrown out, although it wasn't given much serious thought either. But then an incident happened in an FA Cup match between Stoke and Notts County and they had no hesitation in introducing 'McCrum's rule'.

However, life for William McCrum was not always a case of wine, roses and sport. His father died in 1915, leaving him a fortune of an inheritance, which he proceeded to squander on flash cars and in the bookmaking establishments of Armagh. The family mill was neglected, fell into disrepair and eventually closed, leaving William bankrupt and almost destitute. He died in 1932, addicted to alcohol, penniless and destitute in a boarding house in Armagh. For almost seventy years, his contribution to the most popular sport in the world was forgotten – until the builders were ready to move in on the historic field.

The field was to be preserved and eventually FIFA, acting on a request from its vice-president, Belfast man Jim Boyce, provided funding to renovate the grave of Mr McCrum in St Mark's graveyard in Armagh city. In 1999, Gary Lineker presented a documentary on the history of the dreaded penalty kick and stood over McCrum's grave and joked that, 'This man has a lot to answer for!' The field on which the world of association football was changed forever is now a public park with a sculpture to William McCrum as its centrepiece. The artwork was created in 2010 by the renowned Belfast artist D.P. Pettigrew and is adorned by informative panels which detail the significance of what occurred on the field.

PRIVATE WILLIAM MCFADZEAN – A PROUD SON OF LURGAN

On the front of Lurgan Town Hall on Union Street in Lurgan is a plaque dedicated to one of the town's most famous sons, Victoria Cross recipient William McFadzean. Born in 1895, McFadzean's act of bravery occurred on the opening day of the Battle of the Somme, 1 July 1916, close to Thiepval Wood, when bombs being opened for an attack slipped back into the trench, which was crowded with soldiers. Some of the safety pins fell out of the bombs, but McFadzean, threw himself on top of them just before they exploded, killing himself in the process but saving the lives of the other soldiers. Private McFadzean was awarded the Victoria Cross for his striking bravery, making him the first to receive the Victoria Cross prior to the actual Battle of the Somme beginning. His citation read as follows:

> For most conspicuous bravery while in a concentration trench and opening a box of bombs for distribution prior to an attack, the box slipped down into the trench, which was crowded with men, and two of the safety pins fell out. Private McFadzean, instantly realising the danger to his comrades, with heroic courage threw himself on the top of the bombs. The bombs exploded blowing him to pieces, but only one other man was injured. He well knew his danger, being himself a bomber, but without a moment's hesitation he gave his life for his comrades.

Private McFadzean stood 6 feet tall and weighed 13 stone. His family moved to the Cregagh area of Belfast when he was still a child and a keen rugby player for Collegians RFC.

He worshipped at the Newtownbreda Presbyterian Church, where a memorial service was held for him on 1 November 1917. A memorial tablet to his memory was unveiled. It bore the words, 'Greater love hath no man than this: that a man lay down his life for his friends'. His Victoria Cross was presented to his father William by King George V at a ceremony held in Buckingham Palace in February 1917. However, eyebrows were raised when William was allowed only the cost of a third-class return ticket from Belfast to London.

DR IAN PAISLEY'S ARMAGH BEGINNINGS

A pivotal figure in the history of Northern Ireland, Ian Richard Kyle Paisley was born in Armagh on 6 April 1926. His father, Kyle Paisley, was descended from Scottish settlers who came to the townland of Brackey in Co. Tyrone in the early seventeenth century. In 1915, Kyle moved to Armagh to work in a drapery store run the Lennox family, who were part of the strict Plymouth Brethren, who did not employ anybody who was not 'born again'. Paisley senior was known throughout the Armagh countryside as a fiery preacher and in 1918 he was invited to become the first pastor of Armagh's twelve-strong Baptist congregation. The congregation met originally in the 'Catch my Pal' Hall on Lonsdale Street. By 1923, he had built up the church congregation to over fifty-four worshippers and married Isabella Turnbull, a 24-year-old railway worker's daughter originally from Kilsyth in Scotland. Both the Paisley and Kyle families had been active in the Orange Order and James Kyle Paisley had been a member of the Ulster Volunteer Force during the Home Rule crisis of 1912.

Their first son, Harold, was born in the family home in Killylea in 1924, which was well known due to its huge biblical mural, which had been painted on the roof for the benefit of passing train passengers. Shortly afterwards, the Paisleys moved to Edward Street in Armagh. The Baptist congregation had donated a house opposite the railway station to the family and Ian was born in that house in 1926. When Ian was 2 years old, the Paisley family moved to Ballymena, where Ian was educated at the town's Model School.

SARAH MAKEM – FOLK SINGER EXTRAORDINAIRE

Born in 1900, Sarah Makem was a folk singer of note. She was the mother of the world-famous Tommy Makem, but she had made a name for herself as a ballad singer long before her son found fame with the Clancy Brothers in the 1960s. She was born on High Street in Keady and married Peter Makem, an accomplished fiddler and flautist, of Derrynoose. They had two sons, Jack and Tommy, and three daughters, Peggy, Mona and Nancy. According to the well-known Belfast singer and folk music historian, David

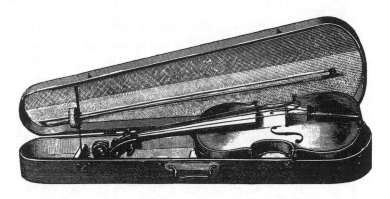

Hammond, Sarah 'was the greatest folk singer in the world' and visitors to her home included Pete Seeger and the poet Seamus Heaney.

Her voice was first heard on the BBC in the 1950s, when she sang the signature tune to the programme *As I Roved Out*. Her musical abilities were honed during her time as a weaver in the nearby Darkley Mill, where she learned many songs and led the women in their singing. She had a repertoire of over 1,000 songs, which she had learned by heart without needing to write down the words. She died in April 1983 and was remembered by the Belfast writer Ciaran Carson as follows: 'She represented a way of life that is vanishing. It was nothing to do with going out to perform in the big concert halls. People came to her to learn and listen. She was held in that sort of awe.'

COURSE LODGE PRIVATE ASYLUM – RICHILL

In 1861, James and William Orr established a 'Private institution for the mental and nervous individuals exclusively for the receipt of ladies' at Course Lodge in Richill, between Armagh and Portadown. The house was supervised by the 'Misses Orr' and provided care and accommodation for fifteen women. In an advertisement in the *Belfast News-*

Letter in December 1886, the asylum claimed to 'embrace all the requisites for the successful treatment of mental malady'.

The advert outlined the advantages enjoyed by patients, who had access to the 'gardens and pleasure grounds' and who were part of a 'home circle' under the supervision of the Orr sisters. In 1901, an inspection of the home found that four of the inmates seemed content as they pursued their needlework in the sitting-room, while one lady was in 'bed for the day, and three more demented cases were in the sitting-room downstairs'. However, criticism was levelled at the owners when 'one lady was found locked in her room':

> She is stated to suffer occasionally from attacks of excitement, during which it is found necessary to leave her in bed and lock the door of her room. This treatment, however, comes within the legal definition of 'seclusion', and should be duly entered in the register; and it will be necessary for the proprietors, in future, to strictly follow the regulations which accompanied the Circular of the 26th May, 1897, with regard to the application of restraint and seclusion.

THE RAPPAREE REDMOND O'HANLON

The original prison in Armagh was situated on Market Street and catered mainly for petty criminals. It was adjacent to McCrum's Court, where underground cells were used also to house the prisoners. One of the prison's most famous inmates was Redmond O'Hanlon, the seventeenth-century outlaw, who was born near Poyntzpass in Armagh in 1640. The O'Hanlon family's lands at Tandragee were confiscated under the Act for the Settlement of Ireland in 1652. The man who inherited the O'Hanlon land was the Anglo-Irish landowner Henry St. John and he soon began to evict O'Hanlon's clansmen from his land. The dispersed O'Hanlons rallied around Redmond and he led a notorious band of highwaymen in and around Slieve Gullion.

Such was his reputation that, in 1674, the authorities in Dublin put a price on his head. Redmond O'Hanlon was murdered on 25 April 1681 by his foster brother, Art MacCall O'Hanlon, near Hilltown in County Down. Art had been bribed by the authorities to carry out the murder and received a full pardon and £200 from the Duke of Ormond for his act of treachery. O'Hanlon's body parts, including his head, were displayed on spikes at Downpatrick Jail. When he was eventually buried, his grave was constantly being desecrated by the duke's supporters. His remains were finally taken secretly by his family and interred somewhere within Lurgan parish.

ARMAGH PRISON

The impressive façade of Armagh Prison dominates the centre of the city and is situated facing the Mall. The construction of the prison began in the 1780s and, during the 1840s and 1850s, it was extended in the style of

Pentonville Prison, which had a central hall with radiating wings, all of which were visible to staff in the centre. The prison in Armagh was designed by Francis Cooley and William Murray and was originally made up of three prisons – one each for women, debtors and those guilty of a felony. Many executions took place both inside and outside the prison. The last execution to take place was that of Joseph Fee in 1904.

Despite its formidable appearance and high security, appeals for information about escaped convicts were commonplace in early newspapers, especially in the late seventeenth and early eighteenth centuries. One particular absconder, Andrew Nixon from Kilmore in Armagh, escaped from Armagh Prison in March 1817 and appeals appeared in papers across Ulster for information that might lead to his recapture. Nixon, it seems, was a formidable character, standing at almost 6 feet (a good 7 inches taller than the average man at that time) and known as a pugilist of note. It would take a brave man to try to apprehend Nixon, despite the small fortune of a £20 reward that was being offered.

£20 Reward

Whereas on the night of Wednesday the 26th inst. ANDREW NIXON of Kilmore, a Debtor, confined in the Jail of Armagh, found means to break out of Prison, and make his escape; he took slates from the roof, and then suspended by a rope which he had secured to the rafters. Whoever apprehends the said ANDREW NIXON, and returns him in any of his Majesty's Jail in the United Kingdom, within six calendar months from the date hereof, or give such private information as may lead to his detection, shall receive TWENTY POUNDS Reward, on application to JOHN TURNER, JAILER.

ARMAGH March 29, 1817

ARMAGH'S MARKET STREET PRISON –
A VIOLENT BEGINNING

We hear from Armagh that two men died there lately in prison, upon each of them were held a coroner's inquest. One of them was a miller, charged with murder by giving a woman big with child a kick on the belly, of which she languished for a time and died; and beating and wounding his own father frequently to the effusion of his blood; the third crime was a by a man committing a vile felony in setting fire to a poor man's cabin and abusing the people inside; the fourth crime was wilful perjury and he died in a very miserable condition.

Belfast News-Letter, 17 May 1739

GOSFORD CASTLE – A ROYAL RESIDENCE FOR THE COUNTY ARMAGH?

With the prospect of the partitioning of Ireland in 1921, one of His Majesty's subjects in Armagh proposed a novel use for Gosford Castle, which was then on the property market. In a letter to the newspapers, Helena Moore suggested that at that time of political crisis the castle should be purchased by the government and the women of Ulster should be tasked with restoring it as a royal residence in Northern Ireland.

She added that 'our women, who now possess equality of political power, should band themselves together and secure Gosford Castle for a royal residence, since Ireland is the only place in the British Isles which has no home to offer a Royal visitor; even gallant little Wales has Caernarfon Castle'. Such a project would be well within the 'spirit of constructive citizenship' for which the women of Ulster were known the world over. Mrs Moore argued that 'here in the midst of our law-abiding north, could we not set this deal to our desire for the continuation of the great qualities that make for the stability of Empire and all progress?', adding that 'After all, the highest reach of human life is love of order combined with loyalty for the cause of right'. Sadly for Mrs Moore, the castle was not purchased by the state. It, along with its historical artefacts, was auctioned off to pay the owner's debts.

Gosford Castle lies close to Markethill and was built by the Acheson family, who were granted over 1,000 acres by King James I in 1610. One of the most famous visitors to the castle was the celebrated writer Jonathan Swift, who designed the nature trails within the extensive grounds. In 1819, Archibald Acheson oversaw the building of a new Gosford Castle, which had been designed by Thomas Hopper, who had been employed by, among others, the Prince Regent, the future George IV. However, by the 1870s, the Acheson family was in dire financial difficulties and the 4th Earl of Gosford, Archibald Acheson, who was a personal friend of Edward VII, was forced to settle a gambling debt by selling the contents of the castle's library.

The castle remained a financial burden to the earl and, in 1921, it was sold at auction, along with its contents, thus breaking the Gosford family's long connection with Markethill. The castle was used during the Second World War as a prisoner-of-war camp for German prisoners and also acted as a base for American troops. For some time after that, it was home to archives belonging to the Public Record Office of Northern Ireland and it was used as a base for troops during Northern Ireland's troubles in the 1970s, during which decade, strangely, it was used also as a base for a travelling circus.

THE LOST TRUMPETS OF
EAMHAIN MACHA

In July 1992, a search was launched for the three missing bronze trumpets that were part of the history of Navan Fort (*Eamhain Macha*). The creation of the company 'Navan at Armagh', whose remit was to resurrect the site as a tourist attraction, gave rise to a call for the return of the three missing trumpets, which had been discovered at Loughnashade near the site in 1798. One of the 2,200-year-old trumpets had been preserved in the National Museum in Dublin, but it was thought that the others were lying in vaults or in the hands of private collectors. Navan Fort had been the capital of Gaelic Ulster. The 'Macha' in the Irish name ('Eamhain Macha') refers to the goddess after which Armagh (*Ard Mhacha*) is named. It was thought that two of the ancient trumpets had been given as gifts to local soldiers by the landowner, Farmer Pooler, and that the other had been stolen. Alas, the three missing trumpets remain lost, but the fourth can be seen in the National Museum in Dublin.

GULLIVER SETS OFF ON HIS TRAVELS IN ARMAGH

In 1999, a priceless first edition of *Gulliver's Travels*, which had been annotated by Jonathan Swift, was nearly stolen from the Armagh Public Library. Said to be irreplaceable, the book had attracted scholars from across the world, who had come to see the unique artefact, which had been on display in a glass cabinet. Also taken during the raid were two ceremonial maces dating back to the 1600s. They had been used by Queen Elizabeth II at a ceremony in 1995, when city status had been bestowed on Armagh. It was believed that the antiques were 'stolen to order', but the criminals were unable to sell them on the black market, such was the publicity surrounding the robbery. The two silver maces were eventually discovered in Balbriggan, County Dublin, while the prized first edition of *Gulliver's Travels* was returned anonymously and is on display in the 240-year-old library.

THE CRAIGMORE VIADUCT

One of the most striking landmarks on the Dublin–Belfast railway line is the Craigmore Viaduct, a railway bridge 2 miles outside Newry which is known locally as the '18 Arches'. Work on the bridge commenced in 1849. It was designed by John Benjamin McNeill, who was born near Dundalk in 1793. The quarter-of-a-mile-long bridge, which was opened in 1852, spans the Camlough River and contains eighteen arches, the highest measuring 126 feet, making it the tallest viaduct in Ireland. When it was opened, the journey time from Belfast to Dublin was greatly reduced and passengers only had to change trains once, in Drogheda. The journey became a direct route with the opening of the Boyne Viaduct in 1855. The Craigmore Viaduct is 1,561 feet long and is constructed of local granite and its workmanship remains a testament to the engineering talent of McNeill. The cost of the bridge was £50,000 and the first uninterrupted passenger journey from Drogheda to Portadown took place on 13 May 1852.

Work on the viaduct was dangerous. On 6 November 1851, 23-year-old John Hollywood, a labourer employed on the project, fell 64 feet from the bridge and died after suffering horrendous head injuries. At the inquest, several work colleagues stated that Hollywood 'had placed himself in a dangerous position from whence he was thrown'. The company was cleared of any wrong-doing and a verdict of 'accidental death' was declared.

NAME CALLING FALL-OUT OVER THE 'LOST CITY OF CRAIGAVON'

In 1967, the foundation stone was laid in a green field in North Armagh for what was to become the new town of Craigavon. The Craigavon Development Commission was appointed in October 1965 to develop the 'new city'. About 6,000 acres of land between Lurgan and Portadown was vested from farmers at a disputed cost of £6 an acre. Forty years later, a 2007 documentary by Newton Emerson entitled *The Lost City of Craigavon* charted the decline of the new town and served as a damning indictment of a plan that never really came to fruition. Initially, the proposal to create a new town was welcomed as a sign of a new and progressive Northern Ireland and it was part of Prime Minister Terence O'Neill's vision in an era of revolutionary town planning, which foresaw the development of 'mixed' housing, cycle paths and all-too-evident roundabouts. Conceived as a linear city along the lines of Milton Keynes, the development was based on similar projects which had proved successful in attracting economic growth. The initial estimate for the cost of the project was £140 million. However, as with many ideas in Northern Ireland, the concept of the city of Craigavon was soon dogged with controversy.

The decision to name the development in honour of Sir James Craig, the first prime minister of Northern Ireland, did not receive the support of nationalist politicians. In Stormont, Austin Currie told the gallery that the 'new city in County Armagh, has not a pup's chance in hell' of success, adding that the government had bungled it by naming the new city Craigavon. He pointed out that the nine-member commission appointed to help run the new city was 'packed' with Unionists. However, criticism of the choice of name came also from Sir George Clark, Grand Master of the Orange Order in Ireland, who stated that there were many beautiful Irish names in the area: 'How much more pleasant would it be say one was going to Lisnamintry or Clanrolla, than to Craigavon?'. 'The whole project had been the pipe-dream of a planner', he added, and he stated that he did not think it should be given 'an illustrious name' (such as Craigavon) when it had no great industry and when nobody

knew where the population of 100,000 was to come from. Another Unionist, Mr V. Cooke, thought it showed great disrespect for a great man (i.e. Craigavon) while the *Belfast Telegraph* demanded 'Rename this Child'.

The dream that Craigavon would become a model town was effectively destroyed when Northern Ireland endured its troubles in the 1970s. Newton Emerson's *The Lost City of Craigavon* explored how one of the biggest social experiments in the history of Northern Ireland had ended in failure. A Portadown native, Emerson commented:

> I suppose I had the attitude that many people in Portadown have towards Craigavon – that it was just a couple of bad estates on the edge of Lurgan. [...] Personally, I now think it was a crazy idea, though a very interesting one. I think Craigavon was the product of something which was very much of its time – cities like it were being built all over the world during the 1960s. [...] As a child, I didn't notice the failure of Craigavon. The new city was an enormous playground of hidden cycle paths, roads that ended suddenly in the middle of nowhere and futuristic buildings standing empty in an artificial landscape. It had a magical quality.

BESSBROOK AND THE QUAKER LEGACY

The term 'Model Village' is quite an apt description of Bessbrook, which is nestled neatly in the hills of South Armagh, approximately three miles north-west of Newry. Bessbrook owes its foundation to a Quaker by the name of John Grubb Richardson (1813–1890) who established a flourishing linen industry in the village and was famed for refusing a baronetcy from Queen Victoria on the ground that, as a Quaker, he believed that all men should be equal.

The village owes its name to Elizabeth (Bess) Nicholson, who was married to Joseph Nicholson whose family owned a linen mill in the district from 1806 until 1845. In 1839, Nicholson's Mill was destroyed in a fire that resulted in the deaths of several of the workers, with the *Freeman's Journal* noting that no trace was discovered of 'one individual who still remained in the burning fabric'.

In 1845, the property was put on the market and purchased by the Richardson family. Linen from Bessbrook famously adorned the tables of the Savoy dining rooms and indeed of the famed *Queen Mary* on her maiden voyage. However, it was the far-reaching philanthropy of Richardson that endeared him to the folk of Bessbrook. He built the village on the principles of social welfare and temperance. Bessbrook millworkers were, unlike their counterparts in the mills of Belfast, very well catered for in terms of medical care, but not so in their ability to purchase alcohol. The overarching principles of Richardson for his model village were 'no public houses and no pawn shops', therefore, in theory, no requirement for police.

In June 1867, the *Birmingham Mail* carried a feature on the village of Bessbrook, which noted:

It remains to say, that there are three institutions which Bessbrook does not possess. It has no public house within its precincts, no police, and no gaol. The Irish Constabulary, we are told, are armed and occupy every other town in Ireland and have barracks for half a dozen men each along every roadside, but there are none in Bessbrook; for there is no drunkenness, no quarrelling, though the inhabitants are all Irish, no theft, no crime, no infanticide – in short, the operatives are models of sobriety and good order. As a result, the homes of Bessbrook are said to be all happy homes, the houses are scrupulously clean, the wives neat and comfortably clad and the children well fed and healthy.

Such was the success of Richardson's social experiment in Bessbrook that, in 1882, Prime Minister William Gladstone wrote to the entrepreneur informing him that Queen Victoria wished to confer on him a baronetcy. Richardson, however, wrote back declining the offer, stating that as a Quaker 'the only reward he expected or wanted for having helped his fellow man, was the pleasure it gave him'.

Today, the layout of the settlement remains the same as it was in the 1880s, with local granite stone adorning the original streets, terraces and squares. When the mill finally closed down in 1972, the premises became the fortified home of the British Army within the eye of the political storm that was South Armagh during the most recent Troubles.

2

PAUPERS, POVERTY AND FAMINE

THE 'PAUPER MENACE' IN ARMAGH

The well-known quotation from Matthew 26:11 reads, 'The poor you will always have with you'. This adage was particularly true in the eighteenth century in Armagh when the poor – or the 'pauper menace', as it was known – was a cause of great debate. Many in society were unsympathetic to the poor, the destitute or the 'idle'. It was seen a personal failure to be poverty-stricken and charity was not always forthcoming. Yet, as far back as 1757, the 'parishioners of Armagh' were noted for their attempts to contain and address the problem of the poor, as the following notice from the *Armagh Guardian* on 17 February 1757 illustrates:

THE Parishioners of Armagh have entered into a voluntary Subscription Monthly, to support the Poor of said Parish, so as they may be enabled with their own Industry to keep House. And all are to take Notice, that no Foreigner or trolling Beggars will be served in said Bounds after the 29th of this Month, but the Law put into Execution against all sturdy Beggars.

In some cases, particularly when poverty was encountered in tragic circumstances, society did what it could to assist the needy. Take the case of Terence Maguire, a poor 15-year-old boy, the son of a widowed pauper, who was working in a flax mill in Tandragee in 1812, when he became trapped in the machinery and had 'both his arms shattered and cut off at the shoulders'. His life was saved but in that period employee liability insurance was non-existent. An advertisement for charity was placed in the *Belfast News-Letter* on 14 February of that year, addressed to 'A Humane and Christian People'. Maguire's life, despite his injuries, had been saved by surgeons Patton and Barclay in Armagh Infirmary and he was soon reported to be in health, but the plea for help pointed out that the boy was 'completely helpless' and that his widowed mother was unable to cope.

The case of Thomas Maguire was, however, a singular example of a concerted effort to assist a pauper who had suffered a tragic accident. Sympathy was in short supply for those paupers who were considered to be of a 'worthless character' and a drain on resources. In 1818, 'A Traveller' writing in the *Belfast News-Letter* commended the city of Armagh for its plans for the 'total suppression of street begging'. The writer pointed out that the city fathers had decided to introduce plans that would deal with the 'aged, infirm, blind and cripples', which numbered 120 individuals. Key to the plan was to levy a charge on gentlemen, shopkeepers and the clergy. The money collected would be used to establish poorhouses where rooms would be provided for the destitute of the city. Paupers with large families were expected to work for their allowances. They were to be provided with lime for the internal whitewashing of their dwellings and fresh straw was to be given to them on a weekly basis to keep insects at bay. The introduction of these measures was said to have had a positive impact within a number of months. According to 'A Traveller', many visitors to Armagh had commented that the paupers 'seemed to be more industrious and cleanly and more decent in their general manners'. In conclusion, the authors suggested that the scheme was 'to the honour to Armagh and the comfort of its inhabitants'.

However, street begging persisted and measures to address the problem were soon introduced at an official level. In 1836, the English Poor Law Commissioner, George Nicholls, arrived in Ireland and compiled a report which proposed the establishment of workhouses like those in England. His bill, which was introduced in the House of Commons on 1837, was entitled 'A Bill for the More Effectual Relief of the Destitute Poor in Ireland' and it became law in 1838. The bill divided Ireland into 130 Unions, each based close to a market town and funded by a levy (or the 'poor rate', as it was known) and managed by a Board of Guardians who were answerable to the Poor Law Commissioners.

In 1840, Armagh Workhouse was built on a 7-acre site at Tower Hill, to the north of the city. Originally designed to cater for 1,100 inmates, it was granted approval to admit paupers in December 1841, the first of whom arrived in January 1842. The workhouse was considered a place of last resort for individuals who were destitute. Men, women and children were totally segregated, families were split up, regulations were strict and food was simple and inadequate. Although Armagh Workhouse was the largest in Ulster, it was soon unable to house all those seeking help, especially in the aftermath of the failure of the potato crop in Ireland in 1845 and the ensuing famine. It was estimated that over 400 individuals died of infection in the institution between October 1846 and March 1847. Life for those in the workhouse was cruel and those who entered the workhouse but were found not to be in dire straits were met with scorn. The *Freeman's Journal* reported one such case in 1849, when 'it was discovered that a woman, who, with her family, had been relieved at the Armagh Workhouse on Saturday night [1 September] was found to be in possession of seven sovereigns'.

The county's other workhouse in Lurgan was opened in 1841, on the grounds of what is now Lurgan Hospital. Lurgan itself doubled in size between 1821 and 1841 and the famine caused a further increase in population. Initially, the workhouse was of a makeshift nature, with many huts and tents serving as dwellings for the poor. In May 1847, it was reported that mortality rates in the workhouse were on a par with the death rate in Ballina Workhouse in famine-torn County Mayo, with over half of the 581 inmates dying between October 1846 and March 1847. By November 1847, the death toll had reached almost 1,200.

The Starving Paupers of Armagh
The *Nation* newspaper of 13 March 1847 contained the following report:

> It is stated that nearly 400 paupers have died in the Lurgan workhouse during the past eight weeks. In Armagh there is some dread that mortality will spread beyond usual limits in the workhouse there. Typhus fever has appeared, and the medical attendant is ill at present of the disease. On Wednesday, the remains of fourteen of the paupers were lying in the dead house.

Armagh Beggars in the Moy

On 15 January 1847, the *Belfast Newsletter* featured the following:

> So greatly is the town of Moy infested with beggars, that some of the inhabitants have been obliged to remove the knockers from their doors. These vagrants are so arrogant and imperative in their demands, that the town may be said to be in a state of siege.

Black '47 in Armagh – Death by Starvation

Reports of starvation appeared in the *Armagh Guardian* on 1 January 1847:

> The Coroner, Mr George Henry, held an inquest on the body of a man by the name of Tomlinson from Tartarghan, who, along with his wife and three children, had instead for months on scraps of food given to them by farmers. He and his family had nothing to eat for days before his death but kale and turnips. Tomlinson had been 45-years-of-age and had been strong and healthy before winter.

TYPHUS FEVER IN ARMAGH

After two outbreaks of the dreaded typhus fever in 1814 and 1815, the epidemic spread across Ireland again in 1817. The number of people who contracted the fever was so great that a hospital was established to treat those suffering from the epidemic at Killuny, a mile outside Armagh. Within a month, almost 600 cases had been treated and sixteen deaths had been reported. The fever did not respect class boundaries and one of the most prominent victims was the Reverend Samuel Close of Elm Park, who was rector of the parish of Tynan. Described in the *Freeman's Journal* as 'a pious and truly benevolent divine he is universally mourned as a public loss to society'.

The fever was, however, short-lived in Armagh and by early 1818 the city was declared free of the malady. In the *Belfast News-Letter* of 3 February 1818, a notice was published which read: 'The city of Armagh is so free from typhus fever at present, that the fever committee are enabled to shut up the fever hospital. Fever still continues in a considerable degree in the country for some miles around Armagh, but is much less prevalent than formerly.' Periodically, the fever returned to the city and in 1845 it was reported that an inquest had been carried out on a man named McNally who had been found dead in the city. It seems that the vagrant McNally had been expelled from a lodging house after the other inmates discovered he had been suffering from the fever. Police and a doctor were called to the house, but McNally was found dead in a vacant house, having died within an hour of his removal from the house.

The fever appeared again in Armagh in 1847 and the most prominent victim on that occasion was Charles Brownlow, the 1st Lord Lurgan, who had served as MP for Armagh at Westminster from 1822–1832. It is believed that Lord Lurgan contracted the fever during a visit to the Lurgan Workhouse and died within thirteen days of being diagnosed. He had gained a reputation for being deeply interested in improving his estate and had been active in trying to alleviate the suffering of the people during the famine, when he had been the chairman of the Lurgan Board of Guardians. He was aged 54 when he died in April 1847.

KEADY INVADED BY DESTITUTE LABOURERS – MAY 1847

The coming of the Great Famine impacted greatly on the vicinity of South Armagh, with bands of unemployed and starving labourers roaming the area, posing a threat to the towns and villages. With public works schemes unable to cope with the levels of unemployment, large numbers of destitute men invaded the town of Keady on the night of Monday, 10 May 1846, in search of food. The inhabitants of the town locked their doors, so the men went first to the soup kitchen, where they tried to break open the door. The local constabulary arrived in force and dispersed them, only for the the mob to return and loot a number of shops. Eventually, representatives of the local relief committee arrived and placed those who were considered to be the neediest on their books. Many of the paupers were taken to Armagh. The committee's intervention prevented serious disorder in the town.

EMIGRATION OF PAUPERS

On 3 June 1846, the *Freeman's Journal* featured the following:

> On Monday, twenty-two paupers left Armagh Workhouse for Belfast to embark in the Bellina for Quebec, sent by the board of guardians of the union. The emigrants were very comfortably clad, and otherwise equipped for their journey.

POTATO BLIGHT IN ARMAGH – ELECTRICITY TO BLAME?

During the potato blight, the sight of fields withering as the disease took hold was distressing and there was much conjecture about the cause of the blight across Ireland. Many believed that the blight had been sent by God, while others tried to blame the events on a natural disaster. The following was written by 'an Armagh Gentleman' who felt that the cause of the blight was electricity. It was published in the *Ulster Banner* on 22 August 1846:

It is truly distressing in this neighbourhood. Our markets are daily glutted and there are few carts in which tainted potatoes are not to be seen. I have observed several fields in the vicinity of the city, all in the most beautiful bloom last week and giving hope of a most luxurious crop; but in a few days they became withered as if the keen frost of October. One field in particular – Cork reds – was green and health looking on Wednesday, and the succeeding Saturday evening the same field had one half as if burned away, while the other side exhibited the same appearance. This shows that electricity must have been the cause, and if any doubt existed on that subject, it should cease when the fact is known that scarcely a night passes that there are not continuous flashes of lightning and, in some cases, light beams ogling along the earth like balls of fire. Many farmers were in great hope that the late crops were safe; but one with whom I was in conversation with yesterday told me that all his crop was discard.

ALARMING ASSEMBLAGE AT MARKETHILL

The *Armagh Guardian* of 5 January 1847 contained the following report:

Last Wednesday 'a multitude of poor looking men and boys' from the townlands of Folio, Cashel and Ballymacnok, which are part of Lord Charlemont's property, came to MARKETHILL and went to the bread shops. Mr Cummings gave them bread so they left the shop without doing any harm. A number then rushed to Mrs James McConnell's shop where they demanded and took what loaves and biscuits were in the shop. They went into several other shops and were refused and then on the way down the street, a wooden draper persuaded them to go home telling them they would be helped.

ARMAGH LEADS THE SURGICAL WORLD

In January 1849, Armagh became one of the first places in Ireland to host a surgical operation performed under the anaesthetic chloroform. The 'useful agent', as surgeons described the chemical, had first been used by Edinburgh surgeon James Simpson in November 1847, yet opposition to the use of anaesthetics remained widespread. The procedure in Armagh was carried out in the workhouse on a man who had his gangrene-infected forearm removed. Far from suffering pain, the man was reported to have been in a 'most agreeable state during the operation' and made a full recovery. It seemed that surgical experiments under chloroform were reserved for paupers in Ireland at that time.

In December 1848, it was reported that a successful operation had been carried out on a pauper in Magherafelt Workhouse, County Derry. The man, Patrick Keenan, spoke throughout the operation in language that was 'quite unintelligible' and was surprised to note that he had lost his leg after a two-minute procedure. Strange as it may seem, Armagh Workhouse was, in 1849, a world leader in medical and surgical science as the use of the chemical on persons of 'good standing' only became widespread after Queen Victoria was sedated during the birth of her eighth child, Leopold, in 1853.

POPERY IN THE WORKHOUSE

In 1859, the visitation of Protestant ladies to the Armagh Workhouse to read the scriptures to the sick and infirm led to a letter of protest from the Catholic chaplain, the Rev. James Campbell. The Board of Guardians dealt with the complaint in January of that year and considered also a request from the priest that nuns from the Sisters of Mercy be allowed to preach to the sick and infirm. As a stout defender of the Catholic inmates of the workhouse, Campbell objected to instances where the Protestant ladies had preached to Catholic children without his knowledge. While the rules of the workhouse had technically been violated by admitting the ladies, Sir James Stronge, future Conservative MP for Armagh, objected to any notion that the nuns should be admitted to the premises. The board opted, however, for a pragmatic solution in the face of a potential religious fall-out by ordering the master of the workhouse to advise the Protestant ladies that they were no longer permitted to preach to the inmates and that the nuns would not be allowed into the house either.

It was not the first time that the Rev. Campbell had come into conflict with the Board of Guardians of the workhouse. In June 1853, a report was brought to the board which claimed that the chaplain had told several Catholic children in the building not to read the Bible since it was 'a book written by the Devil or an evil spirit calculated to make Roman Catholic children Protestants when they grow big'. It was reported that 'eleven of the priest's pauper flock when examined by the board, agreed, with slight variations, in this description of the priest's language'. One by one, the Catholic children, aged from 8 to 18, were brought before the board and each of them affirmed that the priest had told them that the Bible should not be read.

The board then considered a letter from twhe Rev. Campbell which outlined his objections to Catholic children in the institution being forced to receive Bible instruction from a Protestant schoolmaster. He quoted regulation after regulation and, despite the board expressing concern about the comments made by the priest about the Bible, they were forced to accede to the priest's request that Catholic children should be no longer obliged to receive Bible lessons. the The Rev. Campbell, it seems, was quite militant in his defence of Catholic children in the workhouse. Three months prior to the Bible-teaching incident, the board had received a complaint that he had baptised some children, claiming them for the faith.

THE BUSY RAT CATCHERS OF ARMAGH WORKHOUSE

In Armagh Workhouse, neither the residents nor the rats were assured a long life. In 1877, inmates at the institution caught 1,717 rats, while, in 1888, it was reported that 795 rats had been caught by the official rat catcher. Such was the gratitude of the Board of Guardians that they awarded the rat catcher a sum of £2 for his diligent work. The

figure of 795 dead rats, although remarkable, was not as impressive as the previous year's total, when the board had awarded a sum of £3 to the then official rat catcher.

3

A PROUD SPORTING HERITAGE

THE SPORT OF KINGS IN THE ORCHARD COUNTY

Horse racing, or the 'Sport of Kings', was a pursuit long associated with the Mall in Armagh and it drew many thousands to city. On Friday, 19 October 1818, a crowd of over 50,000 descended on the city for the Armagh Hunt races, where the 'ground was laid with great judgement, and carefully measured by the stewards' on duty. It was reported that the 'fashionable and the poor' had attended in abundance, but, thankfully, the day passed without much drunkenness or disturbance as the spectators 'dispersed to their respective homes highly gratified by the amusements of the day'. The main race of the afternoon was for the Armagh Cup, which was won by Mr William McDermott's grey mare, Waterloo. McDermott's horse romped home over the 3-mile course in just over nine minutes, leaving the pre-race favourite, 'Trough Raider', in his wake. The event took place just four years after Wellington's victory at Waterloo, so the name of the battle was very much in vogue; the next race, 'The Waterloo Stakes', was won by Mr Edward Moore's 'Timekeeper'. The favourite, 'Poor Simpleton', finished in a disappointing fourth place, much to the annoyance of the crowd.

While the day's racing in 1818 was relatively free from trouble, the authorities always feared sectarian violence as the crowds dispersed in a drunken state. In 1834, the racing in Armagh was marred by 'a great deal of rioting with many bloodied heads as a consequence'. That evening, a 'crowd of ruffians' returning from the races attacked the home of a Protestant man who was forced to fire his shotgun in defence. The mob then turned their ire on a Protestant man and his daughter who were walking home from the nearby hospital. The girl was beaten senseless. The father and daughter survived, after intensive treatment, and, at the Armagh Assizes in March 1835, their near neighbours, John Macklin, Daniel Connery, James Finn and Audy Hughes, were found guilty and transported for life to Australia.

ROYAL 'SPORT' OF COCKFIGHTING

One of the most popular 'sports' in pre-Victorian Ireland was the royal sport of cockfighting. It was a pursuit of the upper classes – or 'Gentlemen', as they were described – and inter-county matches were played out in various locations. One of the earliest recorded cockfighting competitions in Armagh can be traced to 9 July 1768, when the birds of Thomas Harden of Mahon took on those of Charles McCue of Armagh in a competition with a grand prize of 100 guineas. The competition took place over four days, with Tuesday and Thursday designated as 'Ladies' Days', and the fighting took place amid dancing and singing competitions. For the privilege of partaking in the talent competitions, any performer not from Portadown was to pay an entrance fee of half a guinea.

In Dublin, contests were held usually in farmsteads or at the Cock Pit Royal on Essex Street on the south side of the River Liffey. Such events could attract crowds of upwards of 500 and the fights were an occasion for excessive gambling,

abundant drinking and inevitable disorder among those in attendance. On Friday, 28 May 1813, the 'Gentlemen' of the County Armagh travelled to St Stephen's Green to face the 'Gentlemen' of the King's County (Offaly) for a Grand Stag Match, at which the winnings were '20 Guineas a battle'. The final contest of the day would see two roosters fight it out for a prize of 1,000 guineas. Amid the poverty in the streets of Dublin, such prize sums were, with hindsight, obscene, to say the least.

The sport, despite being banned, thrived in the rural parts of Ulster, especially in Armagh. On Wednesday, 29 March 1930, a crowd estimated to be 1,000 strong gathered at Ellis's Cut, close to Lough Neagh, for an illegal cockfight. The RUC arrived on the scene prior to the commencement of the battles and ordered the drivers of two buses to return to Belfast, leaving the Belfast contingent stranded. The crowd then reconvened at Maghery, where they were again frustrated by the police. Undeterred, the fighting enthusiasts crossed Lough Neagh by ferry to County Tyrone, where they were once again intercepted by police, who had been waiting for them.

SCHOOLS' CUP RUGBY IN ARMAGH

In Ulster Schools' Cup rugby, the undisputed kingpin of County Armagh is the Royal School. The school won the inaugural competition in 1876 and went on to win seven of the first ten finals. However, from 1885, the school endured a run of poor luck in the competition and it wasn't until St Patrick's Day of 1977 that the pupils again enjoyed a day out at the final in Belfast's Ravenhill ground. In what was described as a 'fairytale encounter' in front of 12,000 spectators, Armagh was victorious over Regent Grammar of Newtownards, thanks to a dropped goal four minutes into injury time by out-half Noel Cummings, which earned him the man-of-the-match accolade.

By winning the cup in 1977, Armagh became the holders of the 'new' schools' shield, which had been donated by the Board of Governors of Methodist College. The Royal School claimed the premier prize in Ulster schools' rugby again in 2004, when they defeated Campbell College by 14 points to 5. Lee Ruddock got the opening try for Armagh that afternoon while centre Ethan Allen added a second, with conversions by Jonathan Gillespie sealing the win. That victory secured the Royal School's ninth title, making them the fifth most successful school in the history of the competition. Apart from the Royal School, no other school from Armagh has claimed the Schools' Cup. In 1934, Lurgan College battled their way to the final, seeing off Portadown College, Bangor Grammar and Coleraine Academical Institute in the process. However, the final proved too challenging for the Lurgan side; they lost by six tries to no score against the mighty Belfast Royal Academical Institute.

JOE COBURN – HEAVYWEIGHT BOXING CHAMPION FROM MIDDLETOWN

Born in Middletown in 1835, Joe Coburn won the world heavyweight championship in 1862 when the reigning champion, John Heenan, refused to box him. That disputed title was then claimed by Mike McCoole in 1866, after the Armagh man had temporarily retired from the ring. In 1864, with Coburn in possession of the disputed title, a match was organised between Coburn and the world-famous Jem Mace for 1 October. Coburn had been termed 'The Adopted Son of America' and in the build-up to the clash with Mace, he had beaten Joe Goss, Tom Allen and Bill Rayel, three boxers Mace had requested that he box in order to prove that he was worthy of taking Mace on in a title bout. However, the tantalising prospect of an Ireland versus England take-all bout was scuppered when Mace failed to show up, even though the purse was £1,000 for the winner. The problem for Mace was the chosen venue – Powerstown in Tipperary. Mace was reluctant to fight in rural Ireland and a huge crowd was left disappointed when Mace decided to forego the clash.

Prior to the fight, Coburn had raised money by hosting a string of exhibitions throughout the British Isles. Described as being somewhat crude and 'unscientific', Coburn visited his native Armagh in July of that year and was feted by the great and the good of the city in the Charlemont Arms Hotel. It was reported that massive crowds turned out to see their champion and he was wined and dined by many 'respectable gentlemen' of the Armagh elite. It was said of Coburn that:

> He is a son of a respectable tradesman, a stonemason who held a farm on or near the Bondville Estate [near Middletown] who emigrated to the United States some sixteen years ago. Joe is himself a bricklayer by artistic

profession and latterly kept a tavern in Now York, which he disposed of to advantage that he might contend with Mace. He is a handsome young man, about twenty-nine years of age, measuring five feet ten inches high, and weighing 13 stone. In conversation Joe is pleasant and gives evidence of education and of having mixed in high society. But there is nothing affected in his language or dress and not the remotest appearance to the fop.

The two rivals, Mace and Coburn, did fight in the ring competitively in Mississippi in 1871, but a winner could not be decided upon and a draw was declared after a battle that had lasted almost four hours in the driving rain. Upon retiring, Coburn was drawn into a life of crime. He served six and a half years in Auburn Prison for shooting two policemen in 1877. Sadly, Coburn spent his final years suffering from alcoholism and living in virtual poverty. He died aged 55 of 'consumption' on 6 December 1890. While he had spent many years in prison during his decline, his place in boxing history was secured in 2013 when he was inducted into the International Boxing Hall of Fame under the 'pioneer' category.

JIMMY JONES – A RECORD-BREAKING GOALSCORER

Born in Keady in 1928, Jimmy Jones made an impression as an outstanding goalscorer with Belfast Celtic in the late 1940s. On 27 December 1948, Jones was attacked at Windsor Park by a group of the home Linfield supporters on a day that has been judged one of the blackest in the history of Irish football. As the final whistle blew, a section of the crowd invaded the pitch and dragged Jones onto the terracing, where he received an unmerciful beating. In the first half, he had been involved in a collision with Bob

Bryson, the Linfield centre-half, whose ankle had been broken as a result. An announcement about Bryson's injury was made to the packed crowd at the interval, which sealed Jones's fate after the game. Despite receiving a career-threatening broken leg, Jones recovered and signed for London club Fulham, eventually returning to the Irish League with Lurgan side Glenavon. He later played for Northern Ireland.

In the 1956/57 season, Jones scored a record seventy-four goals when Glenavon achieved the league and cup double. Football was not his only passion. He was also an enthusiastic motorcycle racer and was seen frequently competing in the Ulster Grand Prix. In all, he played 517 times for Glenavon and was their leading goalscorer for ten successive seasons between 1952/53 and 1961/62. His career goal total was 646 for his various clubs and he is still the record goalscorer in Irish League history. At Mourneview Park, the home of Glenavon, a suite is named in honour of Jimmy, who captained the club during its tour of the USA in 1960 and managed the club from 1969 to 1972. His honours include three Irish League championship medals and three Irish Cup medals. He also won three caps for Northern Ireland.

PORTADOWN WIN THE GOLD CUP – 1933

Hailing from Shamrock Park, Portadown wore many guises on the football field before entering senior football in 1924. They achieved their first major honour on the afternoon of Wednesday, 6 December 1933, when they defeated Glentoran at Cliftonville's Solitude ground to claim the Gold Cup. Portadown had qualified for the final after a victory over their close rivals Glenavon, which was followed by a win over Cliftonville and a semi-final victory over Distillery on 1 November. The final saw special trains booked from Armagh and Portadown to ferry over 3,000 fans to Belfast's Great Victoria Street station, where trams were lined up to ferry the supporters to the ground. In the event, 7,000 fans saw the mid-Ulster side emerge victorious by a goal to nil. The vital goal was scored by William Johnstone with three minutes left to play. That night, massive crowds greeted the team upon their arrival in the town and marching bands paraded the team through the market square where a bonfire was lit in celebration. The historic 1933 Portadown team was made up of: Lawson, Clarke, Ewing, Cochrane, Bullick, W.K. Johnstone, Gourly, Sinnamon, Hart, Johnston, M'Cart and Smith.

By winning the competition, Portadown became only the second club from outside Belfast to claim the trophy, following Shelbourne's victory in 1915. Portadown went on to retain the trophy in December 1937 when they beat Belfast Celtic 2–0 at Distillery's Grosvenor Park during a torrential downpour. The scorer of Portadown's decisive second goal that day was 17-year-old outside right David Cochrane, who left the club for Leeds United within two weeks of the final, swelling the club's coffers with a £2,000 transfer fee.

Portadown's most successful period occurred in the late 1980s and early 1990s. In the 1990 season, the club broke the 'Gypsy's Curse', which was said to have been placed on Shamrock Park when they won the Irish League for the first time. The following season, the club retained the league title and rounded off a fabulous year when they beat their bitter rivals Glenavon in the Irish Cup final to secure the club's first league and cup double.

GLENAVON DO THE DOUBLE 1956/57

Footballing glory came to the town of Lurgan during the 1956/57 season, when Glenavon secured the Irish league and cup double. By doing so, they became the first team from outside Belfast to achieve that feat and their historic achievement was secured on 13 April when the 'Lurgan Blues' defeated Derry City in the Irish Cup final at Windsor Park. In that final against Derry City, before a crowd of 23,000, disaster struck for the 'candy stripes' left-back and captain when he put the ball past his team's goalkeeper, Charlie Heffron, scoring an own goal. That goal, two minutes from time, was followed by a second by the irrepressible Jimmy Jones in injury time, which secured the trophy for Glenavon. Later that year, Glenavon became the first team to represent Northern Ireland in the European Cup, but they were knocked out by Aarhus of Denmark in the first round on a 3–0 aggregate score.

MID-ULSTER FOOTBALL ASSOCIATION

At a meeting of local association football clubs in Armagh city on Saturday, 2 April 1887, it was unanimously agreed that clubs from Armagh, Monaghan and Tyrone would be welcome to apply for membership of the Mid-Ulster Football Association. The meeting was attended by clubs from Clones, Darkley, Loughgall, Milford and Monaghan town. It was agreed that the principal aim of the body would be to promote the game of association football in the vicinity. Membership of the association was set at 15 shillings a year, with a one-off joining fee of 10 shillings. The clubs represented agreed to apply for membership of the Irish Football Association in Belfast, with a view to competing in the Irish Challenge Cup. Clubs were to be encouraged to apply for membership to the honorary secretary, William McCrum of Milford, whose club won the first ever Mid-Ulster Cup Final the following year, in 1888.

LURGAN'S GAA KINGPINS

The Clann na nGael club from Lurgan were most certainly the kingpins of Ulster club football in the early 1970s. Formed in 1922 on Francis Street, the club has been very successful over the years, but recently it has, like the rest of the club sides in Armagh, been eclipsed by the all-conquering Crossmaglen Rangers. The Lurgan side's success in the late 1960s was built on a strong ethos of teamwork. The team came to prominence in the county when they won the minor crown on three successive occasions from 1965–1967. The club went on to win the county senior title in 1968, which they retained the following year. In 1971, the Lurgan side lost the Ulster senior club final to Bellaghy of Derry, but won the provincial crown the following year when they saw off Tyrone champions, Ardboe. That particular year's Ulster championship was notable because 'Clann' played Glasgow in the opening round tie in Scotland, which was the first time that a club championship game had been played outside Ireland.

In the 1973/1974 season, Donegal side St Joseph's were beaten in the Ulster final, resulting in an all-Ireland club decider against University College Dublin. The final was played on St Patrick's Day in Croke Park as the current raiser to the Railway Cup hurling final. The Lurgan side were confident of securing the cup, having eight Armagh regulars on their side, including future all-Ireland captain, Jimmy Smyth. The game ended in a draw of 1–6 a side, with Ollie Leddy of Cavan saving the day for the students by scoring a late equaliser to send the tie to a replay. However, it was not to be for the 'Clanns' in the replay on Sunday, 28 April, as the university side became the first Leinster winners of the title when they defeated the Lurgan side by 0–14 to 1–4 at a windswept Croke Park.

When talking about sides that have brought glory to Armagh in the world of GAA, it would be remiss not to mention Crossmaglen Rangers. In 1997, the club lifted the all-Ireland club title in Gaelic football when they defeated Knockmore in the final on St Patrick's Day. Between 1996 and 2015, Rangers won the Armagh crown every year, with the only blip occurring 2009. During that period, they won eleven Ulster Senior Club Football titles and they won the all-Ireland crown six times (1997, 1999, 2000, 2007, 2011 and 2012). In all, Rangers have won forty-three county senior titles, which is twice as many titles as that of their nearest rivals, the Armagh Harps. In 2016, the champions were denied a seventh successive Armagh title when they were beaten by a point by Cullyhanna in the semi-final by 1–15 to 0–17.

IT NEVER RAINS BUT IT POURS – CROKE PARK 1977

In the 1977 final, despite scoring 3–6, a feat that could have won many previous all-Ireland football finals,

Armagh succumbed to Dublin by 12 points. The captain of the Armagh team, Jimmy Smyth, was later to blame 'the overawing sense of occasion' as a huge factor in Armagh's defeat to the reigning champions that day. With nerves fraying at the edges, the Armagh team decided to leave their dressing room early to warm up on the Croke Park pitch and they were greeted by a tremendous roar from the massive crowd there to support them. While the Dublin team sat composed in their changing room, a downpour of epic proportions fell on the Orchard County players on the field of play. When Dublin entered the pitch ten minutes later, the sun had appeared and Armagh's players could only watch, drenched to the skin, as the 'Dubs' made their way confidently towards Hill 16 to greet their fans. As Jimmy recalled, 'We were naive and inexperienced while Dublin were appearing in their fourth successive final. Armagh appeared on the pitch much too early and were soaked before the game got under way; the Dubs had a more patient approach.' The heavy downpour that fell on the Armagh men was a sign of what lay ahead that afternoon. Despite losing the final, the team returned as heroes to Armagh city the following evening and they were greeted by a cheering crowd of 25,000 at the Athletic Grounds.

2002 ALL-IRELAND FINAL: ARMAGH, AT LAST!

For supporters of Armagh's senior footballers, Sunday, 22 September 2002, was redemption day as the pain of the defeats in 1953 and 1977 were erased forever at Croke Park. The Orchard men had battled their way to an Ulster title in July that year with a well-deserved win over Donegal, capping off a campaign which had seen them dispose of Tyrone and Fermanagh in the earlier rounds. In the championship proper, Sligo were disposed of after a replay at the quarter-final stage and Dublin were defeated by a single point in an epic battle at Croke Park on the first day of September. Having watched fellow Ulster sides Down, Derry and Donegal claim the Sam Maguire Cup in the early 1990s, Armagh braced themselves for a clash with favourites Kerry in front of an 80,000-capacity crowd as history beckoned.

By half-time, the game was seemingly going according to form as Kerry had established a solid platform to claim their thirty-third title, leading by 4 points, 0–11 to 0–7. The Armagh team had the added disadvantage of playing into a stiff breeze after the break; that was when manager Joe Kernan decided to take destiny into his own hands. The pain of the heavy defeat to Dublin in 1977 was still raw for Joe, who produced his loser's plaque from that game. He outlined to his players how worthless the plaque was to him in comparison to an all-Ireland medal and hurled it against the wall, breaking it in the process. If ever the Armagh players needed to know what was required in the second half, they knew then.

For star forward Oisín McConville, Kernan's action energised him for the remainder of the game. Despite having missed a penalty before the break, McConville put in a legendary display to see Armagh over the line. With fifty-three minutes gone, Kerry still lead by 4 points, but failed to register a score again while Armagh, thanks to a goal from McConville, convinced their supporters that history could be made. A point by Ronan Clarke in the fifty-ninth minute was duly followed by another from Stephen McDonnell in the sixty-third, to edge Armagh into the lead. But McConville's decisive goal finally occurred in the fifty-fourth minute, when he buried the ball home after a move started by Andy McCann. Armagh clawed back to level four minutes later, when Clarke zipped over a cracking point from the left and McDonnell gave them the lead with another. Armagh kept that one-point lead as Kerry crumbled in the face of a determined outfit that denied a score in the last twenty minutes. Joe McKernan's legendary and damaged plaque is displayed in Croke Park's GAA Museum. The Armagh side that day was made up of Brendan Tierney, Enda McNulty, Justin McNulty, Francie Bellew; Aidan O'Rourke, Kieran McGeeney, Andrew McCann; John Toal, Paul McGrane, Paddy McKeever, John McEntee (0–1), Oisin McConville (1–2), Stephen McDonnell (0–3), Ronan Clarke (0–3) and Diarmuid Marsden (0–3). The subs were Barry O'Hagan and Tony McEntee.

THE PAIN OF 'THAT' MISSED PENALTY

Prior to the elation of 2002, fans of the Orchard County would recall the year 1953 with pain as it was the year when Armagh lost to Kerry in the final before a record crowd of 85,155 in Croke Park. It was said that over 90,000 people had been crammed into the stadium when the entrance gates had been broken open for this novel pairing of teams from north and south. The final captured the imagination of Ireland and Armagh were slight favourites for the title after claiming the Ulster title by defeating reigning provincial and all-Ireland champions Cavan. The nucleus of the Armagh side was composed of the team which had won the 1949 all-Ireland minor title when they defeated Kerry.

It was the match that would haunt Armagh football for many decades. One incident of bad luck was blamed for Armagh's defeat. With Armagh behind by 2 points, 1–5 to 0–10, Bill McCorry was fouled by Kerry's goalkeeper John Foley and referee Peter McDermott awarded a penalty. McCorry missed the penalty and Armagh's moment of glory was postponed for forty-nine years. Sadly, Bill McCorry, despite being one of the most feared attackers in Gaelic football, carried the burden of the man who had cost Armagh the 1953 final for many years. Fittingly, the man-of-the-match trophy for the Armagh senior county football final each year is dedicated to the memory of Bill McCorry. The cup is presented by McCorry's club, Derrymacash Wolfe Tones. Speaking in 2013, after the county final, the Wolfe Tones' coach Patsy Magee said, 'Wolfe Tones are honoured to be involved with this award on a yearly basis. We are very proud to be representing the McCorry family who donated this award. Honouring Bill in this way is fitting, considering his contribution to both the Tones and Armagh.'

BULLETS IN SOUTH ARMAGH

Road bowls, or 'long bullets', is a sport which thrives in two counties in Ireland, Armagh and Cork. It was traditionally played all over the country and was said to have been brought to Ireland by soldiers in William III's army and thereafter to have become popular among workers in the local linen mills. The sport is played along the principles of golf, with competitors aiming to throw a 28oz iron ball (perhaps originally a cannonball) over an agreed distance in the fewest throws. It is a game of skill in which the competitor uses speed, control, tactics and accuracy to complete the course enforced by their opponent. The throwers can call on the help of a road guide and a manager in his task and duels can attract upwards of 1,000 spectators on a summer's evening when betting is usually brisk. Traditionally, it has been the preserve of men, but, since 1981, women have had their own championship. The sport has changed little over the centuries and attracts competitors from Germany, Holland and the USA to the by-ways of Armagh as interest in it has reignited. Armagh had the honour of hosting the first ever all-Ireland road bowls championship in 1963, when over 20,000 spectators gathered at the Moy Road to witness the final between Armagh and Cork. Armagh's Danny McPartland was the winner as he finished the 3-mile course, thus beating Derry Kenny, of Cork, on the final shot by just 11 yards.

4

A SEAT OF HOLY LEARNING AND PEOPLE

A LOVABLE CITY OF TWO CATHEDRALS

Armagh is one of the most lovable cathedral cities in the world, fair in its site, its sacred buildings and homes of learning, its air of quietude, culture and ease. The place where St Patrick founded his church and set up his crozier on its central height. In concentric circles round that steep hill are streets of noble buildings – a library and Georgian houses, ivy-clad – and then of fine shops and modest dwellings. These circles go back to the very days of the national apostle; for they stand where, in ancient times, the ramparts of a vast double or triple rath were dug. Radiating streets are Irish Street, Scotch Street and English Street, making the quarters assigned to the nations, a thousand years ago, when a university at Armagh gave hospitality like that of medieval Paris, to all who sought holy learning.

Aodh De Blacam, *The Black North*, 1938

LOYALTY TO ROME – ADDRESS
FROM CITIZENS OF ARMAGH

Prior to the visit of John Paul II to Ireland in 1979, one of the largest outpourings of Catholic faith on the island occurred in June 1932, when the 31st International Eucharistic Congress was held in Dublin. The congress, which had been established in 1881 under the pontificate of Leo XIII, was one of many international gatherings which were held to celebrate the Catholic faith. A vast crowd, which was estimated to have consisted of over 1 million people, converged in Dublin for a final Mass in the Phoenix Park, while a concluding blessing was administered on O'Connell Street by the papal legate, Cardinal Lorenzo Lauri. Such was the scale of the event that a special radio station was established to broadcast the proceedings of the congress. Known initially as Radio Athlone, it would subsequently become Radio Éireann in 1938. Ireland was chosen as the venue for the congress as it would take place on the 1,500th anniversary of the commencement of St Patrick's mission in Ireland.

One of the highlights of the papal legate's time in the country was a visit to County Armagh on 28 June, where he visited the children of Foley National School outside the city and was greeted by a mass of papal colours while the pupils sang 'God Bless Our Pope'. The roads into the city were thronged with well-wishers who, it was reported, had left the fields to greet the noble visitor. Armagh city itself was adorned with papal scrolls and flags, while a large cordon of RUC officers sealed off the Protestant quarter of the town at Scotch Street, effectively hemming residents into the homes. The legate was greeted by Cardinal McRory and soon the crowds broke through the cordons to catch a glimpse of the Pope's representative and many endeavoured to kiss his ring.

Accompanied by the cardinal and bishops, the legate visited the Convent of the Sacred Heart at Mount Street. Afterwards, a special detour was made to allow the cardinal legate to tour the Catholic districts, which were elaborately decorated. Shrines had been erected in the doors of the houses and at the junctions of streets. The cardinal's return route to Dublin saw him visit Keady and Newtownhamilton. In Keady, the entire Catholic population greeted the cardinal, who was led into the town by the Pipers' Band, the members of which were dressed in picturesque Gaelic costumes. Just before he crossed over the border, men working in quarries at Silverbridge rushed to the roadway and waved to the legate until he had gone out of sight over what the *Irish Press* labelled 'the unnatural frontier'.

THE GREAT RELIGIOUS REVIVAL OF 1859

The fundamentalist religious revival, which spread throughout Ulster in 1859, attracted a great crowd to one of the largest ever meetings held in Armagh on Wednesday, 16 September. The 'monster' revival meeting in the city, attended by 25,000 people, was held thanks in part to the Ulster Railway Company, which agreed to carry the 'saints' to Armagh at a very reasonable cost. It was announced on posters throughout Armagh that week that 'great men' would be present and it was advertised that Mr Charles Spurgeon, the 'Prince of Preachers', and Henry Philpotts, the Bishop of Exeter, would be in attendance on the day. As it turned out, neither of the prominent preachers attended, but their names helped to draw the masses from across Ulster and Ireland to the meeting, which was held 'in a gently sloping grass field, a few minutes' walk from the railway station where there was a wide prospect from it over a well wooded country'.

The meeting was a total success. The crowds came principally from Armagh, Monaghan and Belfast. The special trains from Belfast that day were packed with 'saints' who had availed of the cheap ticket price to go to Armagh. On the road to the field, they 'hooted and whistled when hymns were sung, and indulged in profane parodies'. Scores of clergymen addressed the crowds while others preached to small groups in various corners of the field. It was in these small groups that 'the wildest and most incoherent preachers were to be found and the most numerous cases of the "deeply affected" were to be seen'. In one group, a report recounted that 'twenty poor wretches fell on their knees at the feet of an ill-looking, vulgar and evidently ignorant man, who was consigning the entire universe to perdition with extreme energy'. At every sentence, the prostrate creatures groaned and grovelled on the earth, shouting 'Amen' and 'Jesus' repetitively.

THE EVIL OF MIXED MARRIAGES IN ARMAGH

In July 1930, the 'evil' of mixed marriages was the subject of a lecture by the Reverend M.M. Mocran, rector of Armagh and lately Professor of Pastoral Theology at Trinity College, Dublin. Preaching at an Orange service in Armagh, he said he had been 'very pained since he came to Armagh to find so many cases of mixed marriages', a practice which he described as 'intensely pathetic'. In one week, he stated, he had had 'six old men and women up with him for help' for the mistake of having married a Roman Catholic in a chapel. These 'waifs and strays', he added, had married on the spur of the moment and he thought it a very pathetic thing that many, believing they were in love, had changed their religion. It was inevitable, suggested the Rev. Mocran, that sooner or later the decision to become Roman Catholics came back to haunt those Protestants who had sold their souls and even after having spent just a year in Armagh, he could tell them tale after tale of misery caused by mixed marriages.

THE RED MENACE OF COMMUNISM – BUT NOT FASCISM?

Cardinal Joseph MacRory (1861–1945) was always warning his flock of the dangers of a multitude of sins, especially during his Lenten pastoral messages. Apart from cinema-going, gambling, alcohol abuse, modern dress and dancing, the danger of Communism was a favourite subject of his and he railed against the 'blasphemous propaganda' espoused by the Soviet Union. In a message read in all churches in the Armagh diocese in 1933, the 'evils of Communism' were outlined in great detail and the grave impact that the 'Red Menace' could have on the young people of Ireland was made clear to those in attendance:

> New times bring new dangers, and just now our country, like so many others, is threatened with the blasphemous propaganda of Communism [...] I have no fear for the result if our people, young or old, get to understand the nature of this Red menace; if they come to realise that Communism, whatever it may blatantly promise about bettering the conditions of the worker, means a denial of God's existence, a denial of the immortality of the soul and of a future life, and war against the Church and all religion.

Fearing that the gospel of Marx was taking hold in the hearts of Irish Catholics, MacRory urged Catholics to have nothing to do with 'such awful blasphemy', adding that that there was a danger that 'some, more especially young men, may be ensnared before they even suspect what Communism implies and stands for'.

The principled stance against Communism in the defence of Catholicism by the cardinal became somewhat blurred when he nailed his pro-Fascist sympathies to the mast by defending the forces of General Franco during the Spanish Civil War. Speaking in Mullingar in September 1936, the cardinal expressed dismay that the Republican Congress (a pro-Leninist breakaway faction of the IRA) had recently sent a telegram pledging support to the Communist movement in Spain. He said:

> It is a very, very serious matter and, in my opinion, one for the State to take notice and have this question of giving public support not to any ordinary party or any

ordinary movement, but to a movement that seeks to destroy faith in God, faith in Jesus Christ [...] I would like to ask you this: to say a fervent prayer for Spain. Poor Spain! So long a great country and a faithful friend of Ireland, now torn and bleeding and fighting for her Christian life. There is no room any longer for any doubt as to the issues at stake in the Spanish conflict. It is not a question of the Army against the people, nor the Army plus the aristocracy and the Church against Labour. Not at all. It is a question of whether Spain will remain as she has been for so long, a Christian and Catholic land or a Bolshevist and anti-God one.

SUNDAY SCHOOL PROCESSIONS IN ARMAGH

Processions of all sorts were considered 'fair game' for the 'rowdies' in Armagh, as this example of a violent attack on a Sunday school procession makes plain. In August 1880, the Reverend Abraham Ford of Camlough brought his Sunday school children for their annual trip to Armagh, but on their way back to the railway station they were attacked in the Shambles area of the city by a crowd armed with sticks and stones. The day had, until that point, been an innocent outing for the children and their parents. They had visited the cathedral and were accompanied by two bands and banners, which were adorned with religious inscriptions which were 'not calculated to offend any section of the community'.

After enjoying the outing in the grounds of the cathedral, the children processed back through the town, but when they reached the Shambles, a number of men began lobbing stones across the street, injuring members of the band. The Reverend Ford, who was struck twice, pleaded for calm but the attack intensified and showers of stones began to land on the children, who panicked and ran for cover. Several

other members of the procession were also struck and some
of them received horrific wounds. The procession eventually
moved forward, only to come under attack again. The stone-
throwing continued until the Sunday school group reached
the station, by which time police had arrived on the scene
and dispersed the mob. Arrests were made and the attackers
appeared at Armagh Assizes in March 1881, where Sub-
Constable Flannigan described in great detail the 'terrible',
'unprovoked' and 'wanton' violence that the procession had
had to endure. In sentencing the perpetrators, Mr Justice
Lawson said that he was going to teach those involved that
'the law is a schoolmaster' and described the savage attack
as an 'outrage' against innocent children.

OLIVER PLUNKETT, ARCHBISHOP OF ARMAGH

Oliver Plunkett was born in Oldcastle, County Meath, in
November 1629. He studied in Rome and was received into
the priesthood in 1654. He taught in Rome until he returned

to Ireland in 1669, when he was appointed Archbishop of Armagh and Primate of Ireland. In 1670, Ireland was to endure a new bout of religious persecution when the Council of Ireland decreed that all Catholic bishops and priests must leave the country by 20 November. When the Earl of Essex was appointed viceroy of Ireland in 1672, he banned Catholic education and exiled priests. Even though many senior Catholic churchmen left the country, Oliver Plunkett refused to do so. Instead, he travelled the country dressed as a layman, preaching in the open countryside. However, he was eventually arrested on 6 December 1679.

One of Plunkett's achievements as a peacemaker was to persuade the Irish to lay down their arms and accept the amnesty offered by the English viceroy. For this act, he was denounced by Catholic extremists as a tool of the English and a friend of Protestants. At the same time, he was hated by the Protestant extremists for his part in reviving the Catholic religion and was falsely accused of plotting to bring in a French army to drive the English from Ireland. It was a strange alliance between Catholic and Protestant extremists that brought about his death. Accused by Titus Oates of being involved in the imaginary 'Popish Plot', he was arrested in December 1679 and imprisoned in Dublin Castle. The following year, he was transferred to Newgate Prison in London and in June 1681 he was put on trial at the Court of King's Bench after an imprisonment of more than eighteen months, much of which was spent in solitary confinement.

Nine witnesses were found among the archbishop's Irish Catholic opponents, four of them priests, to give evidence against him. He was found guilty of treason and sentenced to be hanged, drawn and quartered. 'The bottom of your treason,' said the Lord Chief Justice, 'was your setting up your false religion, than which there is not anything more displeasing to God or pernicious to mankind in the world.' After the trial, the archbishop was offered his life on condition that he confessed his guilt and accused others, but he refused. The sentence was carried out at Tyburn on 1 July 1681. His body was dismembered by the executioner, but some English Catholics managed to rescue most of the remains. His head is preserved in Drogheda, Ireland, and most of the other remains are in Downside Abbey, England. Pope Benedict XV beatified Oliver Plunkett in 1920 and Pope Paul VI canonised him in 1975. His feast day is 11 July, which was the date of his execution.

KNOCK APPARITION AND CURES IN ARMAGH

The apparition at Knock, County Mayo, in August 1879 caused much hype across Catholic Ireland. For months afterwards, the newspapers were full of stories of miracles attributed to the remarkable events. News of the apparition of the Virgin Mary, St Joseph, St John the Evangelist, a lamb and a cross on the gable wall of the local Catholic church spread throughout Ireland and established the village as a focal point for pilgrims. As thousands descended on the site of the apparition, the parish priest, Archdeacon Bartholomew Cavanagh, began to take note of all the miraculous cures reported to him and they were then published in *The Nation* newspaper. Residents of County Armagh were prominent in the list of those cured. There was, for example, Patrick Green, of Derrynoose, who claimed that he had been cured of blindness in his left eye. Mr Green, it was said, could not 'distinguish his children in front of him' until he washed his eyes in holy water from the shrine. Such was the hysteria created that Archdeacon Cavanagh received thousands of requests to send some cement from the shrine to people hoping for a cure to their ailments.

In April 1880, a Michael McEvoy from Loughgilly, near Markethill, wrote to request some cement from the church, advising the parish priest that a recent pilgrimage to Knock had cured him of his insomnia and he could 'take different types of food that I could not take before [his pilgrimage] – praise be to God!' He then advised the priest that he had taken some cement from the church back to Armagh and that his mother, Mary McEvoy, after applying the cement, had been cured of a long-standing pain in her knee. That was not the end of the cures in the family. A sister, Catherine McEvoy, had been 'cured of a vomiting of blood'. It was explained that, 'She was given up by priest and doctor and received the last Sacraments, when I sent some of the cement to her. As soon as she got some of it, she immediately got relief. She got up out of bed on the next day, and walked to the chapel and got confirmation.' The most curious case in the county was reported in September 1880, when the Lurgan Board of Guardians considered a request from a woman that her child be placed in the workhouse to enable her to undertake a pilgrimage to Knock to have her diseases cured. The request was met with a firm rejection.

CARDINAL SUFFERS A 'MONSTROUS INDIGNITY'

In June 1922, Northern Ireland stood on the cusp of open civil war as sectarian strife gripped the north in the aftermath of the partition of Ireland. Security was tight in the border region, with B-Special patrols mounting checkpoints and civilian searches. However, one particular stop-and-search operation on Thursday, 15 June, caused consternation among the Catholic population and condemnation from the nationalist press. That evening, 82-year-old Cardinal Michael Logue was travelling by car with his future successor, Archbishop Michael O' Donnell, from a confirmation service near Newry to Armagh when they happened upon a patrol of specials.

In what was described as a 'monstrous indignity', the car carrying the cardinal was stopped by the patrol and all on board were ordered to the roadside while the vehicle was searched. Despite being dressed in his full vestments, topped off by an unmistakable red hat, Cardinal Logue was asked his name and address by a B-Special as the vehicle and bags were searched. The chauffeur was requested to take out the car's spare wheel, which was then deflated and searched. After some further questioning, the cardinal and his entourage were allowed to proceed on their way. Cardinal Logue, who was born in County Donegal in 1840, died in 1924 after serving as Archbishop of Armagh for thirty-seven years.

SUNDAY OPENING OF CINEMAS

The moral crusade in Armagh against drinking, gambling and dancing added the evil of the cinema to its forbidden list in Armagh in the early 1930s. It was a cause that united both Catholic and Protestant clergy and led to the closing of Armagh's cinemas on Sundays, but, thankfully for children, Saturday matinees were reprieved. In a Lenten pastoral in February 1934, Cardinal MacCrory condemned, among other things, jazz dancing as 'unworthy of Catholics at any time of the year, not to speak of Lent', and cinemas as 'no place for a Catholic'. The crusade continued in early December when Mr J.B. Hanna, the Commissioner in Charge of Armagh Municipal Affairs, was urged in a meeting with Protestant clergy to ban the opening of cinemas on Sundays. The commissioner indicated that he would indeed ban the opening of cinemas on Sundays from 31 March and that he would be prepared to delegate his powers to a censorship committee, consisting of clergyman from both denominations. The committee would have the power to ban films and would be provided with prescreenings, in order to judge a film's suitability, and they would be also be shown all posters advertising films.

The decision of the commissioner was challenged at a council meeting by two local cinema owners, Mr J. Kelly, manager of the Armagh City Cinema, and Mr G. Harrington, manager of the Armagh Picture House. The council was split, but agreed that the matter would be the subject of a plebiscite, which would take place on 14 March. On the Sunday prior to the vote, a statement was read out at all Masses in Armagh urging all Catholics to boycott the 'evil influence' of cinemas until the cinema authorities made some effort to procure clean pictures. The subject did not capture the imagination of the Armagh public, with only 20 per cent of the electorate turning out. The vote was 302 to 209 in favour of closing the cinemas on Sundays. However, a previous decision to include the closing of cinemas on a Saturday afternoons, when children's film were shown, was overturned by the council.

A SACRILEGIOUS ACT IN TULLYSARAN

With poverty endemic across Armagh during Victorian times, there was an associated rise in crime across the county – some of it rather desperate in character. In June 1861, the Catholic church in Tullysaran, 2 miles from Armagh city, was ransacked by 'some ruffians', who stole six candlesticks, altar cloths and a range of other religious relics. The parishioners were soon on the case and a local named Williamson, who was reported to have countless aliases, was duly pinpointed as the leader of the band of robbers.

With retribution now the principal aim of the mob, Williamson was 'arrested' by an angry group of locals and he was forced to publicly confess his guilt, which he pleaded was due to drunkenness. The crowd was not placated by

Williamson's case and he was soon on the verge of summary justice but managed to escape into police custody thanks to an 'honourable' gentleman who was present. With the police now in control of matters, Williamson led them to the hiding place chosen by the gang, where they found the candlesticks and all the other articles. The following Saturday, he was brought before a magistrate by Constable McGoldrick, who had arrested him, and was committed for further examination.

DANCES AND DRESS SCANDALS CONDEMNED BY CARDINAL

Having survived the 'monstrous indignity' of having his car stopped at a checkpoint, Cardinal Logue soon returned to the battle against the forces which were corrupting the minds of Ireland's Catholic youth. In March 1924, he preached in Armagh against the 'scandals' connected with the dancing craze and women's dress. In addition, he added the 'menace of the cinema' as another corrupting influence which parents needed to guard against as another 'evil'.

His Eminence referred to the traditional modesty of Ireland's women and girls, but warned that their slavish devotion to fashion had damaged a previously honourable reputation. 'The dress, or rather the want of a dress, of women at present was a crying scandal,' said the cardinal. He pointed out that, in Rome, the Cardinal Vicar had recently published a decree permitting priests to withhold Holy Communion from women who presented at the altar in 'unbecoming dresses', a step that he felt should be introduced in Ireland. Dancing was next on the cardinal's roll of condemnation, especially all-night events which had little or no supervision. He stated that he had 'no objection' to dancing, provided the dances in question were old Irish dances and took place at reasonable hours. The character of the imported dances – 'the names of which were bizarre enough', he added – were objectionable to the core. He warned parents that if they allowed their children to be 'exposed to these corrupting influences', then Almighty God would hold them responsible for the consequences.

CARDINAL LOGUE ON GAMBLING

On 10 November 1912, Cardinal Logue preached to his flock in St Patrick's Cathedral on the 'evils of gambling'. Describing intoxicating liquor as 'that one species of bad seed', the cardinal then condemned the 'evil seed of gambling and horse betting being sown by the enemy of souls' among the poor. He stated that he was sad to see that the vice of gambling had taken hold among the people of Armagh, particularly as the younger generation had been affected by the scourge by the bad example of their elders. The congregation was told by the cardinal that he was 'seriously thinking of using the severest censures of the church – even excommunication – to cope with this terrible evil'.

His view was based on five prosecutions for gambling that had been reported in the Armagh area in recent months. He felt that the practice encouraged dishonesty among the working classes of the area. Shopkeepers, he added, had complained that weekly bills were being left unpaid by customers who had spent their money on gambling. He also complained that drinking was freely indulged in by gamblers when they won and used to drown their sorrows when they lost. 'Gamblers,' he suggested, 'could never be trusted by their employers' and, speaking personally, he said he would 'instantly dismiss his servants if they were betting on horses'. While the sermon was delivered with good intentions, the chasm between the means of the cardinal and the means of the working classes, 'who would bet their last tuppence on a horse', was huge.

THE 'BIG FREEZE' IMPACTS ON CARDINAL D'ALTON'S FUNERAL

The 'Big Freeze' of early 1963 impacted greatly on what should have one of the most public occasions ever to have taken place in the city of Armagh. The funeral service for Cardinal John D'Alton took place on 6 February 1963 during the worst snowstorms of that infamous winter and prevented travelling dignataries and local people from attending. Bishops, clergy and mourners were stranded in many parts of Ireland and many messages were received by telephone at Ara Ceoli, the primate's residence, and the parochial house, from people caught in huge snowdrifts on the way to Armagh. The snow-covered streets were almost deserted as President de Valera, accompanied by Cardinal Spellman, Cardinal McIntyre and a procession of thirty cars, passed through on the way to the cathedral. In the streets of Armagh, scores of council employees had worked from an early hour, clearing the road approaching the cathedral. If the chaos caused by the blizzard wasn't severe enough, a power cut occurred during the ceremony and journalists were forced to file their reports from candlelit phone boxes. BBC and RTÉ engineers used emergency generators to ensure that the proceedings were televised. Pews in the cathedral were sparsely populated as the cardinal's body was removed for burial in the adjoining grounds.

5

TALES FROM THE COURTHOUSE

THE EXECUTION OF PHILIP FITZPATRICK, 1848

Events such as public hangings always attracted crowds to Armagh Prison. At noon on Saturday, 12 August 1848, for example, 5,000, 'from whom not a note of pity did drop from their lips', turned up on to witness the execution of Philip Fitzpatrick. Fitzpatrick had been sentenced in May of that year for the murder of two brothers named Michael and John Henderson in a frenzied knife attack in Lurgan. Fitzpatrick was originally from County Cavan but had worked in Lurgan for many years as a 'knacker', or a 'skinner of horses', as the *Belfast News-Letter* described him. However, he was a rogue of dubious morals who had been incarcerated four times previously for offences, all of a sectarian nature. The paper, however, reported that it was gratifying to note that Fitzpatrick had been contrite in the hours leading up to his execution, praying with his clergyman for a full six hours before he met his fate. He was escorted to the gallows, crying out 'Christ have mercy on me.' After a full minute, the bolt was drawn and his body fell into the abyss. It was reported that 'one short quivering motion of his left leg was all the sign of life betrayed by the murderer, and, after hanging for almost an hour, he was cut down and buried in the gaol yard'.

DOUBLE EXECUTION AT ARMAGH PRISON, 1815

In February 1815, Ireland was appalled by news of the murder of Reid Mulholland in Hamiltonsbawn. Reid was attacked with a hatchet as he lay in his bed and soon suspicion fell on his wife, Jane, and a local man named Robert Edgar, with whom she was having an affair. After returning from Belfast that fateful day, a tired Mulholland went to bed only to be awoken by an attack perpetrated by Edgar, who then dragged Mulholland into a laneway and slit the poor man's throat. Edgar made good his escape and Jane Mulholland waited ten minutes until she raised the alarm with her neighbours, many of whom had been aware of her ongoing affair with Edgar. Police searched Edgar's home and found the axe and a gun that he had stolen from Mulholland buried in his garden. Both Edgar and Mulholland were taken into custody and soon the sorry tale of the murder plot was confessed to the police.

At the trial, the jury were told of how Edgar had visited the dead man's father and read the Bible to him just days before he carried out the brutal murder. The judge described the crime as 'a foul, black and deliberate crime' and the jury pronounced a guilty verdict. The death sentence was duly passed and the culprits were both executed on 19 July outside Armagh Prison before a huge crowd. The *Belfast News-Letter* reported the executions in all their gory detail, describing the scene as follows: 'Prisoner Edgar was a very ugly little old man, with a face which seemed to be an odd compound of monkey and goatish features. The murdered man was a good looking young fellow. The adulteress was a remarkably handsome woman.'

BODY SNATCHERS AT WORK IN EGLISH

At Tynan petty sessions on Saturday, before Sir James Matthew Stronge MP, and Colonel Cross, William Prentice senior, and William Prentice junior, were charged at the instance of Jane Anderson with unlawfully and wilfully on the 4th May last, breaking into and entering the churchyard of the parish of Eglish, in the county of Armagh, and with opening a grave in which one William Anderson, deceased, had a short time before been buried, and unlawfully, wilfully and indecently taking away his body. Mr Harris appeared for the plaintiff and Mr. Simpson for the defendants. The bench after hearing the evidence offered on the part of the plaintiff – no evidence being submitted for the defence – held that the defendants had committed a misdemeanour, and accordingly sent the case for trial to the next quarter sessions in Armagh.

The Northern Whig, 1 August 1868

THE EXECUTION OF THOMAS SINCLAIR – ARMAGH PRISON, 1820

The discovery of the battered body of William McKenna in the Callan River in February 1820 led to the arrest of Thomas Sinclair of Derryscallion, near Moy, on the charge of murder. Sinclair had travelled to Swatragh in County Derry, where he had asked McKenna for a loan of his horse and cart to deliver furniture to a house he said he had recently acquired. McKenna agreed and travelled with

Sinclair, but when they arrived at the Callan River, the issue of payment was raised and a fight ensued during which Sinclair murdered McKenna and covered his body in a bog. Later that night, fearful that the body would be uncovered, Sinclair returned and disposed of the body in the river. It appears that Sinclair committed the murder with the assistance of a mute 20-year-old named Tippen. Tippen, with a guilty conscience, had led police to the scene of the crime and Sinclair was duly arrested and sent to Armagh for trial, where he was found guilty and sentenced to death.

The execution took place outside Armagh Prison on 28 July 1820 in front of a large crowd. Claiming that he was innocent to the end, Sinclair 'appeared quite hardened and careless as to his future state' and was attended by his clergyman, the Rev. William Ball, chaplain of the prison. He persisted in asserting his innocence to the crowd as he was ushered to the scaffold, refusing to confess when asked by Ball and blaming Tippen for the crime, together with a man named Menaul, who he said had fled the country. At a quarter to two, Sinclair had the rope placed around his neck and cautiously put one foot forward to meet his destiny. Without fear, he addressed the crowd one final time saying, 'Good people, I am going to die for the murder of William McKenna. I never murdered him, nor do I know anything of the murder; no, I never did and I die innocent! Good people pray for me.' Those were the final words he uttered as the platform was opened and his body fell a distance of 8 feet 'so that to all there was an appearance that he was dead in an instant'.

NO MERCY SHOWN AT THE ARMAGH ASSIZES, 1790

It wasn't much fun being a prisoner before the Armagh Assizes on 4 April 1790, especially when the Honourable Mr Baron Power was chairing proceedings. Take the case of

Bridget McDonnell, who appeared on the charge of 'taking feloniously eleven yards of cotton from the shop of John Brown of Armagh'. The charge was proven and Mr Power handed down a death sentence to the poor woman to be carried out on the morning of 11 May. Sympathy was also in short supply when William Harrison appeared in the dock, his crime being horse-stealing, for which he too was sentenced to death on 11 May. Isaac Lemon fared no better when he was charged under the Chalking Act (i.e. malicious wounding) and sentenced to hang on 13 April. Next up was John Weir, who was convicted of riot and assault, but mercy was shown and he was ordered to be publicly whipped on three occasions.

The execution rate was maintained, however, when Michael Donnelly received a death sentence for the act of highway robbery. As the session progressed, it seemed that Mr Power became more lenient. Michael McCartan appeared charged with stealing lead and was handed down a three-month sentence with hard labour. However, for Catherine Lennon, the act of rapping doors with an infant in her arms, begging for money, was viewed very dimly, with Power sentencing her to six months in Armagh Prison. The severity of the sentences handed down was common throughout Armagh during the 1790s, but one case brought before Lord Chief Baron in August 1792 was strange, to say the least. Standing in the dock that day was one Mary Cooney, who was charged with robbing 'on the King's Highway' a Bernard Kerr of 'a coat, waistcoat, a pair of breeches, a shirt, and a pair of shoes and stockings, all values at 10*s*'. The poor – and seemingly formidable – woman was sentenced to be hanged on 6 November. If he was married, one can only imagine how Mr Kerr explained the loss of his clothes to his wife.

'POCKET-PICKING' IN ARMAGH

Many towns in Armagh were 'infested', as the papers then described it, with the scourge of pickpocketing. Indeed, in December 1841, the *Northern Whig* claimed that an outbreak of cholera in Armagh city had been caused by travelling pickpockets from Drogheda, who had spread the illness to those in whose houses they lodged. The report went on to state that a number of local people had contracted the disease; six had been removed to the local hospital and five of them had since died.

Thursday was market day in Lurgan, so there was always a large crowd and where there was a large crowd, the pickpocket fraternity invariably turned out in force. In April 1887, the market was visited by a gang of pickpockets who mingled with the customers, plying their trade to great effect. One of the victims was a Mrs Hopps, wife of Thomas Hopps, a grocer on Hill Street, who had gone to the butter market carrying a bag containing £4 in silver coins. In the midst of the crowd, Mrs Hopps had her bag opened and the money stolen. The constabulary were promptly called for, but, by then, the pickpocket had made good his or her escape. The problem continued into June, when the market was again visited by a gang of professional pickpockets who 'deftly relieved' people of their money and possessions. The RIC, having been forewarned that the thieves were operating at the market, deployed extra resources. Working undercover, Sergeant Thomas Fairley apprehended one woman, Ann Rogers, with her hand in another woman's pocket. It was found that the prisoner was an expert in the 'light-fingered' trade and she sentenced to two months' hard labour in Armagh Prison.

However, dealing with pickpockets was not always a matter left to the constabulary. In 1873, a Mr Miller from Lurgan discovered that a half-a-crown had been stolen from his pocket while he was visiting Moira fair, near Lurgan.

Determined to trace the pickpocket, he returned to the public house where he believed the money had been taken from him. While standing at the bar, he felt a hand entering his pocket. Immediately, he grabbed the culprit by the throat and accused him of having stolen 10 shillings from him earlier in the day. Threatening to call the police, Miller demanded that the pickpocket return the money to him. The thief at once handed him 10 shillings and made a quick escape, thereby leaving Miller with 7 shillings and sixpence profit for his trouble.

THE DECEPTIVE PALM READER

The appearance at the Armagh Petty Sessions of a 'well-dressed' woman by the name of Mademoiselle Sylvia Carmiene in 1902 caused quite a stir in the city. The woman, who lived in Belfast, had been arrested for 'unlawful use of a certain craft, that is, to examine the hand of a Margaret Leitch by palmistry'. Mr S.H. Monroe, prosecuting for the Crown, quoted the relevant legislation, which specified that any person professing to tell fortunes would be deemed a 'rogue and a vagabond'. He told the court that Madame Carmiene, who claimed to be Ulster's leading palmist, had placed an advertisement in the *Ulster Gazette* in late May, which indicated that anyone who would use her services would be guaranteed 'health, wealth, talents and prospects'. The defendant had read the palms of hundreds of persons over a a period of three weeks in the lobby of the Commercial Hotel, charging a shilling per consultation. Margaret Leitch, a 17-year-old servant girl, described how the accused had told her that she would 'soon have a change in circumstances', but to be careful when travelling on trains. In addition, Leitch was told that she would be going to a 'large building, perhaps a hospital' and, on handing the palmist a further shilling, she was assured that she would be 'married by the age of 23'. Mr Monroe, to the court's amusement, pointed out that the witness had 'paid two shillings, the first of which brought her to the hospital and the second a husband'. Another servant girl told the court how the defendant had told her that 'someone loved her' and that there was 'money coming her way'. Not surprisingly, given the less than insightful nature of her fortune telling, Madame Carmiene had nothing to say in her defence. Perhaps she had already foreseen that she would be found guilty of deception and sentenced to three days in Armagh Prison.

ATROCIOUS MURDER NEAR NEWTOWNHAMILTON

On Sunday, 3 January 1841, six armed men called to the house of Thomas Powell, close to Newtownhamilton. Upon answering the door, a servant girl was pushed out of the way and the men found Powell in the parlour with his two daughters, Sarah and Letitia. The intruders grabbed Powell and quizzed him about a school he was overseeing the building of for the local landowner, a development which had led to the displacement of a number of local Catholic residents. A struggle ensued in the house and Powell was dragged outside, where he was shot in the chest and died. The gang escaped and the murder caused outrage throughout the county.

The police centred their searches on nearby Crossmaglen. They suspected that the murder had been sectarian and had been carried out by Ribbonmen. A breakthrough came when one gang member, Peter Hanratty, had a crisis of conscience – aided no doubt by a generous reward for information – and decided to turn Queen's evidence and implicate the rest of the gang, one of which, Patrick Woods, was tried for murder in August 1841. Hughes had not helped his own cause by attending the inquest on the body of Powell, where he was recognised by one of Powell's daughters and arrested. Hanratty admitted that he had been part of the gang which had travelled to Powell's house on the night of the murder. His evidence was compelling as he described how one of Powell's daughters had cried out, 'Dada, dada, are you going to murder my dada?' Hanratty said that he had already been in prison for stealing fowl and that one of his brothers had been transported to Botany Bay. He claimed that he wanted to save his own neck by telling the truth. The jury found Woods guilty and he was hanged in front of a huge crowd outside Armagh Prison on 20 November.

However, the case did not close with the execution of Woods. One of those implicated by Hanratty was Francis Hughes. Hughes's lawyer was fighting an uphill battle and claimed that the jury, being all male and Protestant, would not give his client a fair trial. Hughes was found guilty. While still in the courtroom, he threw his hands towards the heavens and cried out, 'By the great God who is now above me, I know neither act nor part in the murder of Mr. Powell, no more than the child that is unborn.' Because he had maintained his innocence, Hughes was allowed to plead his case in private to Thomas Powell's son in Armagh Prison prior to going to the gallows, but this appeal was to no avail. Hughes was hanged in front of a riotous crowd of 5,000 outside the gaol on 20 April 1842.

A VERY STRANGE AND UNUSUAL ATTEMPT AT ROBBERY

The sitting of the Armagh Assizes on 29 July 1825 dealt with the peculiar case of Margaret Quinn, who was charged with entering the house of George West of Cornascribe near Tandragee with the 'intent to carry away his goods and chattels'. Described as a 'blooming damsel of about 26 years', Ms Quinn was caught red-handed as she attempted to enter the house by means of a rope which had been dropped down the chimney. Mr West had, however, become alarmed by the noise of someone on his roof in the middle of the night and had waited by his fireplace, pitchfork in hand, to capture the burglar. The sight of the blackened and 'blooming damsel' emerging from his chimney breast may have been one of the strangest sights that Mr West had ever encountered, but he subdued the housebreaker until the constabulary arrived and arrested the dishevelled Quinn. In court, perhaps the feeblest defence ever was pleaded by Ms Quinn, who said that she had entered the house with the consent of Mr West. This, of course, begs the question of why she did not just enter through the door rather than down the chimney, with the assistance of a rope. Not surprisingly, the jury was not convinced by the tall tale and the judge sentenced this damsel to six months' imprisonment with hard labour.

JAILED FOR THE THEFT OF THREE EGGS

In November 1936, the theft of three eggs by Joseph Hamill of Banbrook earned him a month in prison. Charged before Armagh Petty Sessions with larceny 'by means of a trick', Hamill pleaded guilty after it emerged that he had called at a shop and had represented himself as an inspector to the Ministry of Agriculture. With the three eggs having been confiscated for the purpose of a 'test', Hamill left the shop only to be arrested after the suspicious shopkeeper contacted the police.

MAGISTRATE'S STRANGE ADVICE ON HOW TO SETTLE A SOUTH ARMAGH DISPUTE

The term 'the fighting men from Crossmaglen' took on a new meaning in the year 1937 when Major J.D.M. McCallum, the resident magistrate, was hearing summonses at the Crossmaglen Petty Sessions. One case brought to the magistrate's attention was for an alleged assault, with threatening language, in which a number of men had been implicated. In exasperation, McCallum, who had been inundated with similar cases from the district, advised the defendants that if they wished to settle the dispute, to go and have a decent stand-up fight. He pointed out that they could get the police sergeant to act as referee, with their solicitors as seconds. Not shirking his own responsibilities, he volunteered his services as timekeeper. As to the novel proposal, the respective solicitors engaged in the case, Mr O'Connor and Mr Fisher, stated that they raised no objection to the suggestion. However, the plaintiff insisted on pursuing the prosecution against three men and decided to forego the prospect of a pugilistic encounter to settle the dispute. The case was adjourned for three months.

A PARTY SONG CONTEST THAT ENDED IN A BRAWL

Major McCallum's role as a resident magistrate saw him oversee some cases that bordered on the ludicrous. Take this example from 1930, when what was described as 'a storm in a tea-cup' centred on a falling-out between neighbours in Drumcairn. A married woman named Margaret Ann Kelly was charged with instigating a fight with her neighbour, William Lynas, among others. Mrs Kelly claimed that while she was 'peacefully standing at her own door', she was insulted by Mr Lynas, who was cursing the Pope and singing 'The Boyne Water' and 'Derry's Walls' inside his own house across the street. Kelly then claimed that Mrs Evelyn Lynas emerged from her house and called her an 'oul Fenian cat'. A further exchange of insults then occurred which ended with Kelly, so she claimed, being struck by Mr Lynas, Edward Maguire and Edward Cairns.

With matters now completely out of hand, Lynas allegedly asked his wife for his rifle so he could shoot Kelly. Maguire was then said to have assaulted another neighbour, Mrs Quigley, who had come to Kelly's assistance. With the street in a state of uproar, Quigley's husband, Henry, arrived on the scene and was apparently assaulted by Maguire, who had armed himself with a brush shaft. Margaret Kelly's husband tried to make peace by taking his wife indoors, but denied that he had shouted 'Up the IRA' in the middle of the affray, an action, it was claimed, which had only worsened the friction.

However, a different version of events was soon to emerge. Kelly did herself no favours by claiming that she had heard Mr Lynas singing a song which she called 'The Boilin' Water' (and not 'The Boyne Water'). Mrs Lynas described how Kelly had sung the republican standard 'Kevin Barry', before entering her house and pulling her out into the street by the hair. William Lynas denied that he had assaulted Kelly or anyone else. He had been struck from behind, he claimed, and denied cursing the Pope, against whom he said he had no grievance. 'It wouldn't pay him to curse the Pope,' he said, adding that he 'had to go and mix with all religions and he had no time for fighting'.

Mrs Kelly was found guilty as the instigator of the row and fined 1 shilling, with 20 shillings costs, together with being bound over to keep the peace. Mr McCallum, no doubt somewhat dismayed by the details of the case, said the whole affair was a miserable squabble. 'These people had lived for many years on amicable terms and if they had a little more Christianity and a little less social religion they would probably have more peace,' he said.

SHOCKING INFANTICIDE IN RICHILL

In January 1872, a shocking case was reported at Richill. A farm servant girl named Maria McKillop was charged with the murder of her newborn female child. The girl, who was described in court as 'not being of sound mind', had travelled through Richill looking for shelter, but had been unable to find lodgings. The last person she spoke to before giving birth was a man named Wilson, whom she begged to let her stay at his house. He refused and during the night she gave birth to the child, which she threw down an old well, where it was discovered by a farmer the following day. The child was recovered and was found to be clutching some straw and leaves in its hands. McKillop was taken into custody in Richill later that day when the police were informed that she had been seen going from door to door, begging for shelter. A man named Nesbitt took pity on her and allowed her to lie on the stairs of his house and called for a local doctor to attend to her. Dr White informed the police that the girl had given birth and carried out an autopsy on the child, whom he found had 'been born alive, but had died of drowning'. The jury subsequently found McKillop guilty of wilful murder and she was committed to Armagh Prison on the coroner's warrant.

VETERINARY SURGEON AND HIS
WIFE SENTENCED FOR CRUELTY

The extraordinary case of James Coulter Thompson and his wife Agnes became known in early August 1893. The veterinary surgeon lived with his wife and elderly mother in Armagh city, but all, it seems, was not well in the family home. On Saturday, 5 August, police were called to the home after a shooting incident had been reported. There they found Thompson with a gunshot wound to his chest and his wife, who had been shot in the left side of her back. The two were not seriously injured and their wounds were described by a doctor who attended as 'trifling'. Both claimed that the incident had occurred accidently when Mr Thompson was examining his revolver and his wife 'endeavoured to take it from him in a playful manner'. With rumours abounding that the couple had been involved in a botched suicide pact, the police, although still suspicious, accepted that the incident had been an act of misadventure.

The story of the Thompson shooting took another twist in late August, when warrants were issued for the arrest of the husband and wife on the charge of having seriously assaulted Mr Thompson's mother, Margaret. The warrants were issued when police were informed that the old woman had taken refuge in a house next door to her son's after she had been the victim of a serious assault. The police interviewed the old woman and she told them that her son had assaulted her, beating her with a thick rope, striking her on the head and face, and leaving her with black eyes and bruises. Her daughter-in-law, she added, had smashed the furniture and pictures in the house and beat her viciously as she lay in bed. The Thompsons were duly arrested and charged with gross cruelty to Thompson's mother. On 18 October, James Thompson pleaded guilty to inflicting bodily harm on his mother, while his wife pleaded guilty to a lesser charge of common assault. The Thompsons' solicitor, Mr Peel, pleaded for leniency, claiming that his clients had suffered in both professional and social status from the ordeal. The judge, however, discarded the pleas, stating that the law was no respecter of social status and that the prisoners would receive the same treatment as 'poor persons'. Mr Thompson was sentenced to twelve months' imprisonment with hard labour, while his wife received a sentence of four months.

A SHOCKING CASE OF CAT CRUELTY

The Imperial Hotel, which stood on English Street in Armagh city, had been established by Robert R. Loudan in 1880, initially as a temperance hotel. Loudan had built up a successful carriage and funeral director's business in addition to his interests in the hotel. However, in August 1903, the hotel was to become infamous for an act of cruelty committed against a cat by a local man named Felix McArdle. On the morning in question, Mr McArdle entered the kitchen of the hotel and demanded twopence from a servant girl, Julia Whelan. When she refused to pay him, he took off his coat, produced a rope and began twisting it under his arm. He then lifted a cat that was in the kitchen and tied a noose round its neck, slamming it three times against the stone floor. The animal was killed and, before leaving, McArdle told Whelan that he 'he would do the same to her as he did the cat'. McArdle was arrested and brought before Armagh Petty Sessions, where the magistrate, Mr N.L. Townsend, told the defendant that what he had carried out a 'wanton piece of cruelty' before sentencing him to a month's imprisonment with hard labour.

PORTADOWN CRUELTY TO A HORSE

In September 1931, a further shocking case of animal cruelty came before the magistrates' court in Lurgan, when two Portadown men, Leo Larkin and James Creany, were charged with cruelty to a horse. It was claimed that the two men had docked the horse's tail without first administering an anaesthetic and then cut the roof of the animal's mouth in an attempt to cure the horse of the 'head staggers'. The animal died the same night. District Inspector Anderson of the RUC described the case as one of the 'worst cases of animal cruelty he had heard of for a long time'. The amateur veterinary surgeons were fined a total of £2 10 shillings for their cruel act. It seems that James Creaney did not learn his lesson in 1931, as, four years later, he was fined 20 shillings for catching wild birds in a field near Drumcree. A schoolteacher, who was called as a witness, told the court that what Creaney had done 'was not a very nice example to children, who watched the operation almost daily'. Still undeterred, in 1954, Creaney, at the age of 71, was fined 5 shillings on each of eighteen charges for keeping six goldfinches and a grey linnet in his home, allowing insufficient space for them to stretch their wings.

THE CURSE OF DRINKING METHYLATED SPIRITS

The liquor laws in the not-too-distant past were administered very strictly and the lack of tolerance for drunkenness was widespread, especially in Armagh. In the 1930s, the curse of drinking methylated spirits saw Thomas McCrea of Vicar's Hill placed in the dock of the Armagh Licensing Court and fined 40 shillings for being intoxicated on 1 October. Constable Cochrane said that he found the defendant intoxicated and smelling of the spirits 'with almost empty bottle under the table' when he was called to McCrea's home that evening. The defendant denied knowing anything of the bottle and claimed that he had spent the afternoon in a nearby public house. He admitted, however, that previously he had drunk methylated spirits and was found guilty. Also in the dock that day was John George Castles of Scotch Street, who was fined 10 shillings for selling liquor to a drunken person. Constable Watson stated that he saw a drunken man coming out of the premises with two bottles of stout in his pocket. Mr Castles said he sold the man the stout to be consumed off the premises. However, the magistrate took a dim view of the transaction and warned Castles that any future infringement could impact on his liquor licence.

6

POLITICAL STRIFE IN THE ORCHARD COUNTY

THE BATTLE OF THE DIAMOND, 1795

Monday, 21 September 1795, was known as 'Bloody Monday' in County Armagh and was the date on which the Orange Order was founded in Ireland. The victory of the Protestant Peep o' Day Boys (named thus because they usually mounted attacks at the break of dawn) over the Catholic Defenders near Loughgall was commemorated by the founding of the Orange Order in the public house belonging to James Sloan of Loughgall that evening. The battle, which led to the deaths of thirty Defenders, was the culmination of widespread agrarian strife in Armagh between the Catholic population, represented by the 'Defenders', and the Protestant residents, in the form of their own militia, the Peep o' Day Boys.

The battle in September 1795 took place at a crossroads known as 'The Diamond', near Loughgall. Defenders and Peep o' Day Boys gathered and an initial stand-off ended without incident when a priest who had accompanied the Defenders persuaded them to seek a truce after a group called the 'Bleary Boys' arrived from County Down to reinforce the Peep o' Day Boys. When a contingent of Defenders arrived later from County Tyrone, it was reported that they were 'determined to fight' and the Protestants quickly regrouped and opened fire on them. It was, according to William Blacker, a short and decisive battle, in which the Defenders suffered 'not less than thirty' deaths. After the battle had ended, the victorious Protestants marched into Loughgall and in the house of James Sloan they founded the Orange Order, which was to be a Protestant defence association made up of various lodges. The principal pledge of these lodges was to defend 'the King and his heirs so long as he or they support the Protestant Ascendancy'.

Contemporary reports of the battle were scarce, but the following is an extract from a letter by an officer in the 9th Dragoons, dated 26 September:

Monday the 21st at Loughgall, in the County of Armagh, the Peep o' Day Boys and the Defenders had a dreadful engagement, in which 30 of the latter were killed. Our troop here, under the command of Lieutenant Wilkins, and a company of the 9th Dragoons, though seventeen miles from Loughgall, with all the alacrity they have ever displayed, were little more than two hours from the time they were called until they were at the scene of the action. When the instant they appeared both parties dispersed.

The Defenders burnt several houses, and robbed from them bed clothes and linen. There were several hundred defenders there from the county of Louth and from the county of Clare, which proves that they have communication with each other from different parts of the Kingdom. This day again, the troop was called on by Major General Pigot to go to Lurgan, for it seems that the disturbances are not quelled.

Freeman's Journal, 3 October 1795

ARMAGH'S LINKS TO MAYO

The aftermath of the Battle of the Diamond saw the intensification of sectarian strife in the general Armagh area. While 'To Hell or Connaught' was a phrase associated with Oliver Cromwell's way of dealing with the indigenous Irish during the mid-seventeenth century, in Armagh, in particular, that invitation to oblivion was alive and well during the latter part of the eighteenth century. The ongoing sectarian tensions, which were based on economic rivalries among the weaving class, culminated in the Battle of the Diamond near Loughgall on 21 September 1795. With the establishment of the Orange Order, attacks intensified and a widespread campaign to drive Catholics from the North Armagh area commenced. Bands of Orangemen, known as the 'wreckers', targeted many Catholic homes and the state of lawlessness across the county forced the authorities to intervene. In a contemporary speech, Lord Gosford, governor of the county, described the sectarianism as follows: 'A lawless bandatti have constituted themselves judges of this new species of delinquency, and the sentence they have pronounced is equally concise and terrible; it is nothing less than a confiscation of all property and immediate banishment.'

The banishment of the Catholic population from Armagh during that period is estimated to have impacted on upwards of 8,000 people. While many fled to Scotland or North America, Connaught was the destination for the vast majority. The *Dublin Evening Post* of 27 August 1796 reported that Colonel Martin of Ballinahinch Castle, County Galway, had given asylum to 1,000 Armagh refugees on his extensive estate. In Mayo, Lord Altamount of Westport provided £1,000 of his own money to build accommodation for 4,000 souls on his land, while other refugees settled in Ballina, Crossmolina, Newport, Castlebar and Louisburgh. In modern times, many indigenous Armagh names, such as Devany, Devlin and Mallon, are still prominent in County Mayo. The migration of the Armagh population to Mayo established a strong weaving tradition and contributed to the political disaffection in the county, which peaked in 1798, when many Armagh refugees joined with French forces that landed in Killala in August of that year. After the Battle of Ballinamuck in 1798, many Armagh names appeared on the list of rebels for whom a £50 reward would be paid for their capture and imprisonment.

SERIOUS ROW NEAR ARMAGH

The *Freeman's Journal* of 10 March 1810 contained the following report:

A row of a desperate character took place on the 17th February in the townland of Knockaconey, a short distance from Armagh, and that a considerable number of persons have been injured. District-Inspector Jennings, accompanied by Head-Constable Holden and a large force of police, immediately left Armagh on special conveyances, and drove to the place where the row was reported to have occurred. They immediately began to investigate matters. The Armagh constabulary were assisted by the Loughgall police. From the information to hand, it appears that the Grange Protestant Flute and Drum Band had been invited for some time past to pay a visit to their friends in Allistragh. The band had only proceeded the length of the townland of Knockaccney, and when they had reached the house of a man named Patrick Hughes, who came out armed with a pitchfork, and told them that he would not let them go any further, and commenced to shout. In a few minutes a considerable crowd had gathered from the houses in the vicinity. These persons were all armed with spades, pitchforks, shovel, flails, and all the available weapons that could be found. The members of the band remonstrated with them, but all to no purpose, and a regular free fight took place, and a large number of the Protestant party have been injured, the worst being Mathew Killen and William Reaney. A Roman Catholic named Arthur Brannigan has been shot through the hand, the bullet coming out at the wrist. It is said that the laneway near Hughes' house for two hundred yards is practically covered with large stones about all bespattered with blood, and empty cartridges, pellets, and bullets have also been found, and taken possession of by the police.

POLICE BLAMED FOR BONFIRE DEATH

The tradition of lighting bonfires on the '11th Night' to commemorate the Battle of the Boyne was not always the traditional date for the commencement of Orange celebrations. Under the 'old' Julian calendar (named after Julius Caesar), the battle occurred on 1 July 1690, but in 1752 the British government adopted the new Gregorian calendar (named after Pope Gregory XIII), effectively moving the date of the battle back eleven days to 12 July. The revised date for the battle coincides with the date of the Battle of Aughrim in 1691, but gradually the Orange Order accepted the revised date. However, in parts of rural Armagh, the lighting of bonfires on the 1 July continued as opposition to the adoption of a 'popish' calendar remained steadfast. In Portadown on 1 July 1869, a number of children lit a bonfire that soon attracted the attention of the constabulary and, on intervening to extinguish the pyre, a serious riot broke out. The trouble began late in the evening when unarmed police arrived and were immediately attacked by a mob screaming 'Down with Gladstone!', forcing them to retreat.

The bonfire was seen by locals as a traditional event which had been held for forty years, but, undeterred, the police returned and began firing shots in the air to make the crowds disperse. The disturbances intensified and the police turned their guns on the crowd, leaving one person, a youth named Thomas Watson, dead and his friend, a Catholic named Gavin, seriously wounded. The police shouldered the blame for the incident and the funeral of Watson attracted a crowd of over 10,000 mourners to the cemetery at Seagoe. Watson, it was admitted by the authorities, was a totally innocent bystander who had been coming out of a local tobacconist's shop. However, the prospect of serious trouble in the town over the Twelfth of July forced authorities to station hundreds of troops at flashpoint areas. The death of Watson was the subject of questions in the House of Commons and the RIC sub-inspector Noonan came in for criticism, but, thankfully, with the town on a knife-edge, the Twelfth of July celebrations passed off without incident.

ORANGE OUTRAGE IN PORTADOWN 1836

The *Leinster Journal* of Saturday, 12 March 1836, contained the following:

> On Saturday night and Sunday morning last, the town and neighbourhood of Portadown experienced one

of those fierce and lawless visitations in which the Orangemen, the boastful upholders of the law, but the practical violators of it, have so long been in the habit of paying. We do not know whether the expressed will of the King had anything to do with the loyal despisers of His Majesty's authority; but at any rate they behaved with a degree of lawless violence greater than is usual with them. They began shouting 'to hell with the Pope'; and 'Verner forever' [a reference to Colonel Sir William Verner, a veteran of the Battle of Waterloo, and prominent Orange leader whose name is preserved in Verner's Bridge over the Blackwater River, which divides Tyrone and Armagh] and then attacking those who refused to join them. About midnight, an attack was launched on the houses of many of the Roman Catholic inhabitants. Not content with this, they afterwards traversed the country for two or three miles, breaking the windows of almost all the Roman Catholics in their way. About a score of houses, we learn, were thus attacked, some of them being very much damaged. Next morning, Colonel Osborne, Magistrate, and W Hancock, Esq., were very active and five of the rioters have been committed to Armagh gaol.

THE TWELFTH OF JULY IN ARMAGH, 1845

In 1845, tensions were high across Ulster as the annual Twelfth of July celebrations approached and the authorities feared the worst in Belfast, Lisburn, Lurgan and Portadown. In Belfast, it was reported that the main parade was a triumph of peace, while in Lisburn 'all was peaceful and as inoffensive as the playing of young children where not an act, word, or look of offence between either party' was witnessed. However, in Armagh city, it was a different story. In anticipation of trouble, Daniel O'Connell had sent his

'Head Pacificator', Tom Steele, to the city with the duty of quelling any faction-fighting which may have been planned by the nationalist residents, but his trip was in vain as late in the evening serious fighting nonetheless broke out in the centre of the town.

That Saturday morning, six lodges of Orangemen, accompanied by banners and led by fife and drums playing the 'Protestant Boys', marched through the city on their way to Loughgall. On their return later in the afternoon, the lodges took a detour from their planned route and paraded towards the Catholic Irish Street. When the parade arrived at Ogle Street, it was reported that four women threw stones at the marchers, which was taken as the signal for the battle to begin. Police reinforcements led by Sub-Inspector Kelly and a small party of constables arrived in the midst of the battle and rushed onto Dobbin Street, where they found themselves in the middle of a vicious exchange of pistol shots and stones.

For almost half an hour, the violence continued with a level of ferocity not seen in many years and the police attempted to keep the rival factions apart. It was reported that seven persons were injured in the crossfire and one Catholic youth, 'a fine young man, named Boyle', had been killed in the riot. The wounded on both sides were badly cut and bruised. The *Freeman's Journal* correspondent reported, 'it is quite impossible for me to convey to you anything like an adequate idea of the dreadful state of confusion and alarm which prevailed throughout the whole city for several hours'. He added, 'all business was at once stopped; the shopkeepers put up their shutters and people hurried to and fro in great excitement; the cries of the contending parties mingled with the shrieks of women and children and the crashing of windows'. By midnight, it was reported that peace had returned to the streets, but during the late evening several persons were severely beaten as they were leaving the city to go home.

AN ORANGE BANNER FOR AN ITALIAN EVANGELIST

In November 1860, the brethren of Armagh City Grand Orange Lodge 184 voted unanimously to forward its banner to Alessandro Gavazzi, an Italian army chaplain in Giuseppe Garibaldi's army. The sending of the banner was an act of solidarity for 'those British Protestants who are fighting under Garibaldi against Papal tyranny and arbitrary power'. Despite being born a Catholic and training to be a monk, Gavazzi was rejected by the Catholic Church for his 'liberal' views and moved to London, where he became a leader of the city's Italian Protestant population. In the 1860s, Gavazzi returned to Italy and served alongside Garibaldi in the fight for Italian unification and to curb the power of the Pope. Almost 1,000 Irish Catholic men enlisted in the Irish Papal Brigade and fought to preserve the power of the Papal States. Calls for Catholics to enlist were made from the pulpits, while church collections were held across Ireland to finance the brigade. However, such was the devotion of some Armagh Protestants to the cause of Gavazzi that in October 1860 a gentleman in that city did Garibaldi the honour of having his child baptised Frederick John Garibaldi in the parish church.

THREATENING LETTER FROM LIVERPOOL TO AN ARMAGH ORANGEMAN

Being a prominent member of the Orange Order and coroner for the County Armagh was quite an onerous job, especially for Mr Thomas George Peel, who, in July 1881, received a death threat all the way from Liverpool, which caused much consternation among members of the order. The letter, which was headed 'Death Warrant', together with a drawing of a skull and crossbones and a coffin, read 'Death to the memory of Orange Peel! Blood and Death by God, Mr Peel!'

The threat continued, 'As a friend I caution you and tell you that your days are numbered; so prepare for your end is nigh. The bells of Armagh will chime the loss of their Orange coroner.' On the reverse side of the note was written, 'God Save Ireland! To hell Victoria and Down with the Orange.'

The fact was that Peel was known to be a fair-minded coroner but the threat was taken seriously within Orange Order circles. A meeting of the local lodges was convened and a resolution was passed in support of the coroner, which stated that 'in accordance with our Christian character and values [...] we record our utter detestation of the cowardly conduct of the Irish ruffians who descend to such things, and we declare that should any injury if any kind be done to our brother, a system of reprisals will assuredly follow'.

Mr Peel was, though, somewhat of an unrepentant defender of the cause of Protestantism. Speaking in Newtownards, County Down, in 1885, he stated that the morals of the Irish Celtic race were doubtful. He claimed that England had invaded Ireland because 'one Irish king had ran away with another king's wife' and that these 'doubtful morals' were indigenous in the current Irish race. Predicting that a final battle against the Romanists was an eventuality, he told the crowd, 'Put your trust in God, my boys, and keep your powder dry.' He concluded by urging all Protestants to be ready and 'prepared for any emergency that may come'.

DERRY ELECTION CAUSES RIOT IN KEADY

The election of the nationalist Tim Healy to the South Derry seat of the House of Commons on 4 December 1885 was greeted with street parties across nationalist Ulster. Across Armagh, bonfires were lit to celebrate Healy's victory, while in Keady the news was greeted with an impromptu parade led by a nationalist band through the town, which soon attracted the attention of the town's Unionist population.

Hand-to-hand fighting ensued as the band encroached on the Protestant quarter of the town and soon a full-scale riot was in progress. Sticks, cudgels and stones were the weapons of choice as fierce rioting unfolded. One man was cut badly when a stone smashed through a window and hit him on the head. The police eventually restored order by pushing the nationalist crowd back into their own quarter. In Armagh, barrels of tar were set on fire by the nationalists as cheers rang out for the leaders.

LOYAL ORANGE TOAST TO VICTORIA AND ALBERT

The marriage of Queen Victoria to Prince Albert in 1840 was an occasion of great celebration across the British Isles. In Armagh, in particular, the occasion was marked by the signing of a letter to the Queen and her consort, which was unanimously endorsed by citizens at a public meeting in the city. The letter, which was overly long-winded in style and tone, was then placed into the hands of His Grace the Lord Primate, who undertook to present it at the first opportunity to Her Majesty:

Madam – We, the undersigned inhabitants of the ancient city of Armagh, penetrated with feelings of the most devoted loyalty, beg to present your Majesty our unanimous congratulations, on having allied yourself to a Prince, possessed of such mental and moral excellence as his Royal Prince Albert of Saxe-Coburg and Gotha. And we do most devoutly pray, that Almighty God may bless 'the holy estate' into which your Majesty has entered, and render it conducive to the happiness of your domestic life – in which the Sovereign, as well as the humblest subject, can alone enjoy virtuous sympathies and solid enjoyments, on which true felicity can be permanently founded. Loyalty to the throne are the characteristic of the British and Irish people; and it is the good fortune and glory of your Majesty, to have united to that feeling a heartfelt devotion to the person of the beloved Monarch of this mighty empire. In laying our hearty congratulations at the foot of the throne, on the auspicious event which has filled the people with joy, we do fervently hope, that your Majesty's kingdom may continue to be quietly and orderly governed; that the liberties of the people may over rest upon the most secure and lasting foundations; that people may be obtained abroad, as it is at home and that your Majesty's reign may be distinguished, in the annals or the country, by such wise and beneficent measures as will secure to your present subjects, and future generations, happiness and prosperity.

Signed by order, and on behalf of the citizens of Armagh, assembled at a public meeting.

W. Paton, Sovereign

THE INTERRUPTED KING'S BROADCAST, MAY 1935

Nationalists were suspected of sabotage in Armagh when King George V gave his radio broadcast to the British

Empire on 6 May 1935. Many hundreds of loyal citizens of Armagh gathered at the courthouse to hear his message to the youth of the empire. However, it was to be an occasion of much annoyance to his subjects in Armagh as 'interference, which is believed to have been deliberate', ruined the audio of the broadcast, as a loud and persistent 'crackle' and 'hiss' began mysteriously and only ended with the conclusion of the speech. When the bands in London struck up the national anthem, the crackle recommenced, but stopped as soon as the anthem had finished. It is believed that an electrical instrument, connected with an aerial, was being used to disrupt the radio signal from a house in the vicinity and that this effectively ruined the broadcast.

ARMAGH ORANGEMEN CONDEMN EASTER REVOLT

On 15 May 1916, the Grand Orange Lodge of County Armagh held a large and representative meeting of its members in Portadown to consider the events of Easter week in Dublin, where the nationalist uprising had occurred. The indignation regarding what had occurred was palpable and it was moved by Sir James H. Stronge, County Grand Master, seconded by Mr James Irwin, J.P., Deputy Grand Master, and unanimously resolved that:

> We desire to convey our heartfelt sympathy to the peaceable inhabitants of Dublin (of all creeds) in their sufferings and losses by the recent insurrection. We hereby declare afresh our loyalty to the King and to the Empire. We venture, to hope that the lives and properties of law-abiding Irishmen will no longer be endangered in the vain hope of creating a false appearance of unity, and we protest against the absurd suggestion of a portion of

the English Press that this is a favourable moment for the introduction of constitutional changes.

Copies of the resolution were forwarded to the prime minister and Members of Parliament for Ireland, urging them to deal effectively with the rebels, especially at a time of war for the empire, when some had taken the opportunity to attack the rule of law in His Majesty's kingdom.

MARY MACSWINEY'S HOSTILE WELCOME IN MARKETHILL

The Westminster general election of October 1924 pitted the sitting Unionist MP, William Allen, against the Sinn Féin candidate, James McKee. One of the most prominent republicans to canvas for the Sinn Féin candidate was Mary MacSwiney, sister of Terence MacSwiney, who had died on hunger strike in Brixton Prison in October 1920. Ms MacSwiney, an elected member of the Dáil, appeared in Markethill Square on Saturday, 24 October, to address a rally in support of McKee, but her attempt to address the meeting was met with a barrage of abuse. It soon became clear that a majority of those present were of a Unionist persuasion.

Given that it was fair day in the town and that MacSwiney was to speak on a platform opposite the premises of the late W.J. Frazer, the well-known loyalist who had been kidnapped and murdered by republicans, a very large and hostile crowd had assembled, many of whom had travelled to the event in order to give the speaker a hard time. The crowd remained fairly orderly until MacSwiney rose to speak, when it was reported that those in attendance 'lost control of themselves' and although MacSwiney spoke for half an hour, 'scarcely a word could be heard owing to the continuous uproar'. During her speech, MacSwiney was struck several times with apples. Stones and bottles were also occasionally thrown at the speaker. There were loud cries of 'Up England', 'Up the Six Counties' and 'To hell with the Pope' as the address continued and police moved in to usher MacSwiney to her car as her speech came to an end. As her car left, it was damaged as apples, stones and sticks rained down on the vehicle. The mood of the Unionist crowd mirrored the mood in the county; on election day, Sinn Féin's McKee was defeated by Allen by 29,021 votes to 11,756.

BALMORAL DEMONSTRATION: SHOTS FIRED AT ARMAGH STATION

The mass Unionist demonstration against Home Rule at Balmoral on Easter Tuesday, 9 April 1912, attracted tens of thousands to the south Belfast grounds. Upwards of 100,000 Unionists travelled to the event from all over Ireland. The procession was measured as being over 4 miles in length. The newspapers reported that the 'orderliness of the gathering is admitted by hostile critics, and it is noted that hardly a policeman was visible'. However, as the attendees dispersed, the mood began to blacken as alcohol took hold of some of the participants. At Armagh railway station later that evening, when the train conveying the Newry, Hamiltonsbawn, and Markethill contingents was leaving, the situation turned ugly as rival crowds clashed. Many on the train, it was reported, 'were mad with drink and were cursing the Pope' while rival factions rained down similar abuse concerning the British monarchy. With both factions using 'the most filthy expressions', revolver shots rang out from the train and many scattered into the streets of the city. Thankfully, nobody was injured in the gunfire, which could have ended in carnage.

FRAUGHT MEETING OF THE
ANCIENT ORDER OF HIBERNIANS

In the 1930s, the ideological battle within nationalist and republican circles between support for Communism and Fascism was laid bare at a meeting of the Ancient Order of Hibernians in Armagh in August 1934. As the large meeting, presided over by Patrick McKenna of the Armagh branch, began, nationalist sentiment was very much to the fore. Expressions of sympathy were made to mark with regret the recent death of Joe Devlin, former Nationalist MP for West Belfast and prominent member of the order. Resolutions were then passed warning against Communism, reaffirming the demand for a united Ireland and condemning partition as a 'political scar that had been imposed to satisfy the demands of bigotry and existed as a menace to peace between the Irish race and Great Britain'. This resolution, which was backed unanimously, added that the Northern Parliament existed on hatred, supported by subsidies from Great Britain'.

The meeting then turned sour as the issue of support for Ireland's pro-Fascist party was discussed. The National Guard, known also as the Blueshirts, had recently been banned by An Taoiseach, Éamon de Valera. Mr Patrick Nugent, son of the then secretary of the order, James Nugent, was greeted with cries of 'Up the Blue Shirts' when he took to the podium. He said that John Dillon, the national vice-president of the order, was proud to be a Blueshirt, which was greeted with cheers and catcalls. The disquiet in the hall led to a number of scuffles breaking out and the police were called to keep the peace. Criticising de Valera, Nugent aimed a low blow by saying that for such a proud Irishman, it was 'was unfortunate in that he did not bear an Irish name, but a Spanish one was just as good'. His criticism of de Valera was not well received and was met by further interruptions, with Nugent calling his hecklers 'Communists'. He then went on to criticise the IRA, who, he said, 'had big mouths'. By this stage, a near riot was ensuing among the crowd and again police intervened and eventually the squabbling stopped. Nugent stated that people in the north would be better within a united Ireland in the British Commonwealth of Nations and described Freemasonry as a 'danger and a pest' which controlled the government, the police force, the army, and everything else in the Six Counties.

IRA RAID ON ARMAGH BARRACKS

With the IRA preparing to mount its Border Campaign in 1956, Armagh city was to be the scene of a daring raid on the barracks which left many in the establishment red-faced. The raid took place in broad daylight on the afternoon of Saturday, 12 June 1954. Word had been passed to Dublin that all the weaponry would be in the barracks to enable an inventory to be carried out. Twenty members of the Dublin IRA set off that morning and based themselves in a farmhouse just outside Dundalk, 5 miles from the border. It was almost three o'clock on a busy Saturday afternoon when a cattle truck and a car drove into Armagh city, to the gates of Gough Barracks. The timing was perfect as it was when the army least expected a raid. Most of the high-ranking officers were 8 miles away in Portadown at a function welcoming Lord Wakehurst, the new governor of Northern Ireland. Others were on home leave and the usual Saturday pursuits of horse racing and shopping meant that the barracks were quiet and off guard.

As the van pulled up at the gate, IRA man Paddy Ford got out and engaged the sentry in casual conversation about joining the British Army. The sentry called another soldier into the conversation and it was at this point that Ford produced a handgun. It became very obvious to the soldiers that Ford had no interest in joining up. More IRA men jumped from the van and disarmed the soldiers in the guardroom beside the gate, taking the keys to the armoury in the process. Within a few minutes, one of the raiders took up guard duties at the gate of the barracks, resplendent in the full regimental dress of the Royal Irish Fusiliers. The truck was driven into the barracks and reversed up to the door of the armoury. At the gate, the IRA 'sentry' saluted and nodded as other soldiers came and went.

The raiders made light work of the armoury as they loaded the van with an assortment of pistols, rifles, Sten and Bren guns. Within ten minutes, almost 300 weapons had been loaded onto the truck. It was all going to plan and nobody in the barracks batted an eyelid. Across the road, however, a young woman named Mary Elliot was working in her mother's sweet shop when she noticed the goings-on at the front gate. Immediately she became suspicious, especially as the new 'sentry' appeared to be wearing the wrong cross-belt and saluting officers incorrectly. She told an officer who happened to be in the shop that there was something 'going on' at the barracks. He ran to the gate and was duly taken at gunpoint into the guardroom. Miss Elliot was now in a panic and ran upstairs to get a better view. From the bedroom window, she saw the van being loaded up by the strangers and immediately phoned the police. She watched as further soldiers were detained as they entered by the gate. While this was taking place, three lorries full of soldiers arrived at the barracks, but they were waved through by the 'sentry'. When the armoury was emptied, the IRA men clambered on board the truck and departed post-haste. The truck, containing 340 weapons, travelled down Thomas Street at speed and headed out of the city to the border. Meanwhile, the RUC responded to the call from Miss Elliot and ten minutes after the raid had finished an officer arrived at the barracks on a bicycle. It is safe to say that nothing much ever happened in Armagh in the 1950s.

FATAL SHOOTING ON THE BORDER

The IRA's insatiable search for arms continued into 1955 and the B-Specials had been given carte blanche to patrol the border. Rumours spread in early March 1955 that a second armed raid was to be mounted on Gough Barracks in Armagh and the border was effectively sealed on the evening of Saturday, 12 March. That evening, Arthur Leonard, an 18-year-old youth, was driving two sisters home from Keady to Darkley in South Armagh. One of the sisters, Alice Mallon, described how the main road was blocked by a car and, thinking that there had been an accident, Arthur Leonard began to reverse his van. Immediately the van came under attack from armed B-Specials. Leonard was hit by a number of bullets and died at the scene. The two sisters were wounded also.

The war of words began, with the Specials claiming that Leonard had ignored their warning to stop. The reaction to the shootings across Ireland was swift and illustrated the anti-Unionist and anti-B-Special sentiment that existed among nationalists. On the Monday after Leonard's death, a student protest rally was held in Dublin and was led by a banner that read 'Students Condemn Black and Tan Killers'. The *Irish Press*, in an article entitled 'B Men', stated, 'The activities of a force like the B Specials, and especially these night patrols, at an hour when large numbers of people are returning to their homes, are a menace to the people.' Westmeath County Council condemned 'the Black and Tans of 1955', while Eddie McAteer, Nationalist MP for Derry City, said that 'something must be done to protect the public from these over-armed, overbearing, over-excitable and under-intelligent commandos'.

7

MISCELLANEOUS ITEMS OF INTEREST FROM ARMAGH

NEAR TRAGEDY IN RICHILL JAM FACTORY, 1968

In June 1968, the town of Richill made headlines across Northern Ireland when an explosion in the Fruitfield jam factory injured twelve women, who were hit by flying debris. In all, twenty-seven women had been working in the factory when the explosion ripped through the premises, hurling a heavy steam cylinder through the roof, which damaged a building 100 yards away. Two women were seriously injured in the blast and detained at Daisy Hill Hospital in Newry. The blast occurred in the preparing room of the factory, where about thirty women were peeling apples. One witness, Rosaleen Mallon, said:

> We were sitting at the three rows of tables when this explosion went off like a bomb. No one could see anyone else for the steam. [...] Women were screaming, not knowing exactly what had happened. I was flung to the floor and found myself lying under a table with a lot of debris on top of me. Men working in other departments came running to help.

The Fruitfield factory was situated on the main Portadown–Armagh road and was established in the 1800s by Charles B. Lamb, who bought the premises for the production of jams and marmalades, made with the fresh ingredients produced by local farmers. The factory closed in the 1920s and reopened in the 1940s, but cheap foreign imports of fruit in the 1960s eventually forced the business to close in the early 1970s. The factory was a noted landmark in Armagh, with its distinctive chimney, and most homes in the vicinity contained larders adorned with tins labelled 'Fruitfield Preserves'.

DROWNINGS IN THE COUNTY ARMAGH

The people of Portadown have long used the River Bann as a place of recreation and swimming. However, the river has always been a dangerous place in which to bathe and many lives have been lost. In January 1820, the river froze in Portadown and attracted many young children to its banks for the purposes of skating. Late on the evening of 6 January, two young boys were skating on the river by moonlight when they ventured too far, only for the ice to give way beneath them. They fell into the freezing water and were sadly drowned. A massive search operation was launched in the town and their bodies were uncovered the following morning. In nearby Armagh city that year, a similar incident occurred when three boys skating on the ice at Dobbin's Lake fell through the ice into the water and lost their lives.

In 1831, two tragedies occurred within a matter of days in the Bann River, resulting in the deaths of two men who had gone to the water to swim during a heatwave. One evening, John Mallon and his 9-year-old son took to the water for a swim. The father crossed the river with his son on his back. When trying to reach the far side, Mr Mallon got into difficulties because of a cramp and sank to the bottom. His son did eventually reach the bank. Two doctors arrived at the scene and dragged Mallon to the bank, but it was in vain as he had drowned. Mallon left a wife and five young children. The following morning, the body of a 60-year-old man was found mere yards from where Mallon had been found.

In 1849, the River Bann was the scene of the murder of a man named McGurk, who was found dead on 20 December after a drinking session in the house of a man named Bright. It seems that a fight broke out in the house and a number of men who were present took McGurk out to the river in a boat, murdered him and dumped his body in the river. A boatman who was interviewed later by police stated that on the night in question he had heard a splash in the water and remarked to his companion that they would no doubt hear of somebody having been found dead before long.

LOUGH NEAGH BOATING REGATTA

Boating regattas on Lough Neagh at Kinnego Bay near Lurgan were popular during Victorian times in Armagh. Organised by the Lough Neagh Yachting Club, the events drew many thousands from 'mercantile and fashionable society' to the lough shore for the principal event, the First Class Cup. In 1831, tens of thousands gathered to watch the race between R.H. Atkinson's *Bride of Abydea* and J.M. Hill's *Water Witch*. The latter won the cup, in what was described as a 'grand contest'. The regatta, which took place over three days, was an occasion for the aristocrats of Armagh to mingle and, most importantly, to be seen in all their finery.

The main social event that year took place in the Urn Room in the Drapers' Hall in Lurgan, when nearly '100 gentlemen' connected with the regatta and friends from Belfast, Armagh and Portadown 'sat down to an excellent dinner, laid out on most tastefully-decorated tables with evergreens abundant in decoration'. After the sumptuous meal, toasts were made to the Queen, Prince Albert, the royal family, the army and navy, the Lord Lieutenant of Ireland and the linen trade, for which loud cheers rang out around the room.

One of the more popular events was a race between the fishermen of Armagh and Antrim, for which a generous financial prize was donated by the officials of the club. Traditionally, there was also a charitable aspect to the regatta; in 1831, a boat race between local fishermen took place for the benefit of the widow and family of a poor man who had been drowned. Such was the popularity of the regatta that the Ulster Railway Company ran special half-fare trains to Lurgan to accommodate the thousands of spectators from Belfast and County Down. On the final evening, the skies over Lurgan were, by tradition, lit up with a massive display of fireworks.

MYSTERY ARMAGH RELATIVE INHERITS A FORTUNE

In March 1873, one lucky resident of Armagh was in for a windfall. The postmaster of Armagh, John Williams, received a communication from the American government stating that a person named Robert J. McCallan, who had been a native of County Armagh, had died intestate at Darlington, South Carolina, leaving property amounting to about £20,000, which was to be inherited by his closest relative in Armagh. The amount of money bequeathed was worth approximately £12 million in today's terms. It was the task of Mr Williams to 'use such effort to discover the rightful claimant to the property'. A notice to this effect was placed in the postmaster's window, but there is no record of whether the relative was ever found.

'A CRYING OUT SHAME': THE CASE OF MARRIED WOMEN TEACHERS IN ARMAGH

The cause of equal opportunities for women was none too evident at a meeting of the Armagh Education Committee in 1932. The matter drawn to the board's attention was the problem of women taking teaching roles 'with particular reference to those whose husbands have good positions, and to the need of employment for young teachers'. The Reverend S. Mayes said that 'a great deal of dissatisfaction was evident, not only among junior members of the teaching profession, but also the general public, about the practice, which was very general in some parts of the county, of women teachers married to men of good standing and of high salary insisting on retaining their position in the schools'. He continued, 'the committee should discourage the practice, and it would be a good thing if public opinion were roused against a practice which was wrong when so many young teachers were unemployed'. One of the female members of the board, a Mrs Quinn, reminded the members that they had previously passed a resolution that employed women teachers must resign upon marrying, with the proviso that the committee could re-appoint them if they wished. However, the secretary, in defending the cleric's comments, said there was no doubt that the Reverend Mayes had spoken about a 'crying out shame' in certain areas of the county. He added that he had long lists of teachers unable to obtain employment since they had finished training the previous year. He added, 'Quite a number of the employed married women were bread winners, but quite a number had husbands in good positions. It was a matter of getting public opinion against them.' After the concerns were noted, the board went on to pass a resolution, strange as it may seem, to purchase a motor trailer fitted out as a travelling dentist's surgery for use in South Armagh by the education board's dental surgeon.

CLERICAL CRUSADER AGAINST HARE COURSING IN ARMAGH: 'AN INHUMAN PRACTICE'

The twin evils of hare coursing and the opening of picture houses on Sundays were met with strong condemnation by the Reverend A.V. Neill at a service of the First Armagh Presbyterian Church in Armagh in 1932. Insisting that he had nothing against the notions of sport and recreation, he feared that some people were beginning to lose their sense of proportion and that they were also losing a sense of what was decent and what was sacred. The cleric went on to provide a history of cruel sports, citing Roman gladiatorial fights and Spanish bullfights, pointing out that the former was 'Paganism on the one hand' and the latter was 'arid Popery on the other'. Having made this gratuitous point regarding popery, the cleric then turned to the problem of hare coursing in Armagh and the brutalities connected with this 'so-called sport': 'This "sport" was a brutal, inhuman caricature, for in it the basest passions of man were aroused and all the finest qualities degraded.' He called on the congregation to join in a protest against coursing 'as it was a blot on their fair name as a Christian people and must cease'. With the congregation in no doubt of the preacher's attitude to coursing, he then turned to the preservation of the Sabbath day. He described how the Protestant ministers had made a private protest against the two Armagh picture houses opening on Sunday evenings, a practice that had commenced some weeks ago, but, he ruefully said, they had not received a reply to their protest. There were pictures, he said, which no one who claimed to be a Christian should go to at any time, but whatever the nature of a picture, one should not go to see it on the Lord's Day.

The crusade against coursing was widespread in Armagh churches at the time. Preaching in the same church on the following afternoon, the Rev. T.H. Witherow of Markethill again condemned hare coursing, despite admitting that he had in the past enjoyed foxhunting. At the Mall Presbyterian church, the Rev. D. Graham also condemned the sport. In the Methodist church, the Rev. J.W.P. Elliott said that he was a firm believer in the goodness of sport, which was 'an incalculable factor in the development of true manliness'; however, regarding coursing, he asked, 'where was the sportsmanship in witnessing highly-trained greyhounds pursuing a little frightened hare away from its natural surroundings?' He continued, 'This was not sport, but a dastardly degrading practice which one could imagine only possible because it gave opportunities to the betting fraternity to indulge the passion for gambling. [...] Cock-fighting, bull-baiting and bear-baiting were prohibited by law, so let them appeal to their parliamentary representatives to abolish this survival of savagery in their beloved land.'

THE NIGHT OF THE BIG WIND, 1839

The 'Night of the Big Wind' occurred on the day of 'Little Christmas', on 6 January 1839. Known in Irish as *Oíche na Gaoithe Móire*, the storm blew in from the Atlantic and caused devastation across the island. Armagh was particularly badly affected and many houses across the county were devastated by the tempest. In Armagh city, the great chimney beside the gasworks was blown over and the area was plunged into darkness. In Lurgan, the town was described as a 'shattered array of houses, with the suburbs and neighbourhood in desolation, impressing the mind with such sensations as one might feel in visiting a country devastated by some ruthless enemy'. In the Brownlow estate, about 300 mature trees were blown down and Loughgall House 'suffered considerably', with over 200 trees felled and destruction reported throughout the village. In Portadown, it was reported that the wind had been like 'an uninterrupted cannonade'. The residents of the town had been fearful that 'Judgement Day' had arrived. The scene in the town the following morning was described as 'devastation unparalleled' in the annals of the county. It was said that the losses incurred would take 'two generations to make good'. The sight may have was devastating, but the inhabitants of the town, it was reported, were thankful to Providence for the preservation of their lives.

GHOST STORIES – 'A FORM OF CRUELTY TO CHILDREN'

The annual meeting of the Armagh branch of the National Association of Cruelty to Children was held in Armagh on Wednesday, 20 February 1929. The report of the society was read by the local chairperson, Mr W.F.S. Wilkinson, who advised the members that the inspector had investigated twenty-eight cases of neglect in the district, which had impacted on sixty-six children, despite only one case coming before the courts. Welcoming the findings of the report, the High Sheriff of Armagh, Mr A.M.B. Chambre, congratulated the society on its work. However, he condemned the practice of parents and grandparents telling ghost stories to children as a 'form of cruelty, which was to be deprecated'.

THE BOOK OF ARMAGH

The Book of Armagh remains Ireland's most important historical manuscript written prior to the twelfth century. Its 221 pages contain the Patrician documents, principally *Confession Patricil* ('The Confession of Patrick'), which is the main source on the life of Patrick, together with Muirchú's *Life of the Saint*, Tierechan's *Memoir* and the *Book of Angels*. It is believed that he copied the book from the confession written by Patrick. The book was one of the symbols of office of the Anglican Archbishop of Armagh and was kept in the safekeeping of the McMoyer family, who pledged the book to Arthur Brownlow of Lurgan on the eve of his departure to London to give evidence in the trial of Oliver Plunkett. The book was preserved by the Reverend Charles Graves, who succeeded in restoring it in 1846 and discovered that it was the work of the scribe Ferdomnach, who died in AD 846. In 1853, the book was in the possession of Lord John George de la Poer Beresford, the Anglican Archbishop of Armagh, who presented it to Trinity College in Dublin. The book is displayed in the Old Library at the college.

STORMS DUE TO NUCLEAR BOMBS?

The proliferation of nuclear bomb tests across the world in the late 1950s led to the then Church of Ireland Archbishop of Armagh, the Most Reverend John Gregg, coming up with a novel theory for the bad weather suffered in the summer of 1958. That year, crops had been lost due to the weather and the archbishop informed the Armagh Diocese Synod of his view that the weather in Ireland had been impacted upon by the ongoing nuclear experiments: 'I am a man of no technical knowledge on this matter,' the archbishop began, 'yet I cannot help thinking about the terrible weather we have been experiencing. Is it the will of God, or are we in some way responsible through the experiments in nuclear fission and fusion which rend and tear the atmosphere around the globe?' One of the fiercest storms occurred in late September of that year. Crops were damaged, forcing farmers to keep children off school to assist in gathering what was left of the crop in the fields. However, whether the ongoing nuclear testing in the Pacific Ocean influenced the Irish weather that year remains a matter of conjecture.

RABID DOGS IN ARMAGH

The dreaded canine disease of rabies, or the 'Mad Dog Brought Terror', was an ever-present fear among the populace of Armagh during Victorian times. In 1888, a boy named James McGarry, who was 'the son of very poor parents', was bitten by a rabid dog near his home in the townland of Aughanlig, in the Armagh Union area. The boy was treated by a local doctor and returned home seemingly cured, but, sadly, relapsed and died within seven days. In 1892, the pack of hounds belonging to the Armagh Hunt Club was destroyed due to an outbreak of the disease. Three years later, a dog contracted the disease and went on the rampage across farms in the Mullyloughran area, attacking a large number of animals. Two boys, Alexander McKee and Norman Rice, were bitten. Police marksmen eventually shot the dog, together with fifteen sheep and cattle that had been bitten by the dog. At a meeting of the Armagh Guardians that evening, it was agreed that the two boys would be sent to Paris to be cared for by the eminent French microbiologist, Louis Pasteur. In 1885, Pasteur had developed a vaccine which had proved effective in combating the development of full-blown rabies in humans.

The Armagh *Sporting Chronicle* reported in March 1853 the distressing case of a horse that had been bitten by a rabid dog in Keady and had contracted the disease and suffered an agonising death. The horse, which belonged to a Mr McCrum, was working in a mill close to Armagh when his owner noticed that he was sweating profusely and biting and snapping at the other horse on the yoke in a violent manner. McCrum sent for the veterinary surgeon as one of his farmhands fetched a bucket of water for the distressed animal. When the hand approached the horse, he was violently attacked and bitten on the brow, immediately above the eye, while another man was bitten on the hand. The vet, Dr Small, immediately diagnosed the horse with rabies and the horse became wild when attempts were made to capture him. The animal escaped and fled to a nearby orchard, where he went into convulsions and died after becoming entangled in an apple tree.

THE 'GHOST' OF SOUTH ARMAGH

The strange case of Francis Farrelly raised many eyebrows when the Dromintee man appeared at Ballybot Quarter Session in October 1895. Farrelly was sued for £10 damages by James McGuill, who claimed that the defendant had damaged locks on his barn and outhouses, which stood at the rear of his house. Farrelly claimed that he had been searching for a ghost on McGuill's property and had slept in the barn in the hope of witnessing the spectre. Mrs Haratty, McGuill's sister, told the judge that she 'had been bothered by complaints from people in the vicinity about the ghost', which, she added, took the form of a rod or pole at her window in the dead of night. Ghost or no ghost, the judge did not believe Farrelly's spooky tale or his reason for being in the barn and sentenced the 'ghostbuster' to four months' imprisonment.

MADNESS INCURRED BY DRINKING INDIAN TEA

In April 1894, the Chief Secretary to Ireland, Sir John Morley, received a special report from the Inspectors of Lunatics in Ireland, Drs Plunkett-O'Farrell and Courtney, which drew attention to the 'alleged increasing prevalence' of lunacy on the island. Each of the counties studied had shown an increase of the malady, with County Armagh being named as one of the districts which had shown a marked increase. The report stated that during the first half of the 1880s, 339 persons had been admitted to the lunatic asylum, while that number had increased to 421 in the latter part of the decade.

As for the reason why there had been such an increase in the number of cases, the two doctors blamed 'agricultural depression' as a key factor. This ailment, it was suggested, had caused anxiety and worries in rural communities and was added to by a decrease in the availability of nutritional food. Of the 421 persons admitted to the Armagh asylum during the 1880s, 349 were from the farming community. Other causes of insanity were claimed to be hereditary alcoholism, emigration linked to the loss of family members and, most interestingly, the drinking of Indian tea. The report claimed that the drinking of tea from India had been 'injurious' since it was of 'inferior quality' and was 'not brewed, but stewed', causing a form of 'peculiar dyspepsia which leads to general debility of the nervous system'.

A CAUTION

WHEREAS Charles McArea, otherwise King, my apprentice, has eloped from my service on Friday the 13th without any reason whatever, as he has often collected money for me, I do hereby caution the public who may he indebted to me not to pay any debts to the above Charles

McArea, otherwise King, and I am determined to put the law in force against any person or persons who may harbour or employ him after this notice.

Dated at Armagh Nov. 14th, 1789.

A DESERTER FROM THE ARMAGH MILITIA

Deserting from the Armagh Militia was quite a serious offence, especially for 22-year-old musician Matthew Pollard, who went absent without leave in October 1807. His disappearance was publicised in many local newspapers at the time and a 5-guinea reward was offered for information regarding his whereabouts. In order to alert the public to what Pollard looked like, the following detailed description appeared in the notice: 'aged 25 years, five feet four inches high, brown hair, grey eyes, slender body, strong limbs and large feet'. In case that wasn't enough to identify the absconder, the following details were added: 'remarkable thick lips and rather turning outwards, a particular opening between his front teeth and his lower jaw and had on him at the time of desertion a regimental waistcoat over his uniform'. Interestingly, the notice advised the public that Pollard 'speaks affectedly as endeavouring to imitate an English accent'. With such a detailed description, it was probable that Pollard's freedom was short-lived. The disappearance of Pollard was not the only upheaval that the band suffered during that period, as the notice ended, 'Wanted, a Master of the Band for the Armagh Regiment – apply as above'.

TWO GOOD PIGS FOR MY VOTE!

A position on the Pigs Marketing Board must have been quite a lucrative one in the 1930s, as the strange case of James Crawley of Whitecross illustrates. He appeared in court in February of that year, charged with trying to bribe David Johnston of Lurgan in order to secure his vote to elect Johnston to the agricultural body. The bribe that Crawley asked for in a letter to Johnston was 'the sum of £5 or two good pigs'. Not wishing to be compromised by the request, Johnston informed the police, who duly arrested Crawley, and his letter was read out in court. The letter stated that as 'everyone is out to get something, I might as well have something for my vote'. When questioned, Crawley said that the letter was meant as a joke. Joke or not, Crawley was sent for trial, while, Johnston, despite having taken an honourable stance, finished third in the ensuing election.

CHILDREN BARRED FROM ARMAGH PRISON

The plight of the children of Belfast women in Armagh Prison was discussed by the Armagh Board of Guardians at its fortnightly meeting in December 1925. The concern of the Guardians was that children from Belfast were being sent to Armagh Workhouse in order to be close to their mothers, which was incurring huge costs. In response to representations made to the Minister of Home Affairs, Sir Richard Dawson Bates, a letter was read out at the meeting, which indicated that the practice was to cease and that the children of Armagh prisoners would be placed in the Belfast Workhouse in the future. The arrangement for the care of children would see the child in question 'delivered' to the Belfast Workhouse by a police officer and a message would be conveyed by the governor of Armagh Prison to the authorities in Belfast that the mother was to be released one week in advance.

THE WEDDING CELEBRATIONS THAT ENDED IN A RIOT

In 1923, a wedding reception at a house in Portadown attracted the attention of the police, who were called to the house to break up a period of prolonged fighting. Appearing at Armagh Court in January 1924, John McCullough and John McQuade were charged with being 'drunk and disorderly', with the former being discharged and the latter fined 10s 6d, together with a fine and 5s compensation for tearing a police sergeant's coat. Both charges arose over the course of the wedding celebration, at which, according to the evidence given by police, 'the drink was free and in plenteous quantities'. McCullough said that the fighting had erupted as there were 'too many in the house and that they [the guests] were all fighting each other'. Upon entering the celebration of the nuptials, police indicated that they had 'found four men paralytic, and one woman unconscious'. The sergeant added that 'the whole community had been "mad" for a week'.

OUTRAGE AT DONKEY RACES
IN PORTADOWN

The organisers of the County Armagh Agricultural Show in June 1937 incurred the wrath of two ladies who had attended and had witnessed the 'Ulster Donkey Derby', a novelty feature at the event. Given that Mrs Shewell and Miss Entrician, of University Street in Belfast, were the honorary secretaries of the all-Ireland Donkey Protection Society, the race was a cause for great outrage. In their letter to the *Belfast News-Letter*, the ladies stated that 'A more unedifying event we have never seen. Is it not somewhat beneath the dignity of a County Agricultural Show to include such buffoonery in its programme?' The letter continued, 'This amusement can only be classed with similar inanities which used to divert the rustic mind some hundred years ago. Every intelligent person knows that donkeys are unfitted by nature for racing. They are short-winded, and so are caused much distress by being forced to take part in any kind of "sport".' The Donkey Derby had first been included in the show's programme in 1936.

Described as an 'innovation in the programme', the initial race had attracted protesters from the Ulster Donkey Protection Society, who had attended the show and distributed leaflets to the crowds. In defence, the organisers had pointed out that the 'crack jockeys' would ride without saddle, stick, whip, or spurs. However, it seems that the protest was successful as the race was discontinued after 1937.

THE MOUNTNORRIS BRIDE WHO DISAPPEARED

The wedding of Mary Birch from Mountnorris to James McDowell on 10 September 1935 was postponed due to Miss Birch's cold feet on the morning of the wedding. She left the bridegroom disappointed and embarrassed at the altar of the local Presbyterian church. As the guests and anxious relatives waited, it was reported that Mary had disappeared from her home that morning and the proceedings were postponed, much to the embarrassment of Mary's family. It seems that Mary was discovered by her father later that day. After a stern talking-to, no doubt, apologies were issued to Mr McDowell and the nuptials were rearranged for the following Wednesday. Thankfully, the attack of cold feet was a one-off for the bride, who appeared on the second occasion and a previously embarrassed groom was not to be denied his bride. It was reported that the 'happy' couple went on their honeymoon in Scotland and then they left for a life in California, where McDowell's father had an extensive cattle ranch.

GAMBLING AND CHILDREN

In May 1936, a grave warning of the impact of gambling on children in Armagh was provided by Mr R.H. Stephens Richardson, High Sheriff of County Armagh, at the annual meeting in Portadown of the Mid-Ulster Branch of the National Society for the Prevention of Cruelty to Children. In the society's annual report, it was stated that in twenty cases, 934 children had been dealt with during the year. In 310 of those cases, warnings were given to parents and five prosecutions were undertaken which led to convictions. Commenting on the figures, Stephens Richardson said he would like to know whether gambling or drinking had caused the increase in the number of cases. Gambling, he pointed out, was on the increase in a very sad way. Agreeing with his sentiments, Captain J.W. Storey, the organising secretary, said that some of the worst cases were not in the towns but in the country. The terrible, pernicious habit of gambling was becoming worse than the drink.

ASPIRIN AND WHISKEY – A POOR MIXTURE

In April 1935, Joseph Faulkner's defence for being caught intoxicated behind the wheel of a motor car was somewhat strange and led to him losing his licence and incurring a fine of £5. Suffering from neuralgia, Faulkner felt that the best cure was to take a concoction of aspirin and whiskey to ease the pain of his condition. When he was arrested, the Annaghmore defendant claimed that the aspirin and whiskey had not 'mixed properly' and had led to him become disorientated on the road. The van driver informed the magistrate that he had taken six aspirin in Stewartstown, County Tyrone, and a 'little whiskey' in Coalisland to help him drive home. Knowing that he was unfit to drive, Faulkner waited in Coalisland until he felt better, but when stopped by police later, he was deemed drunk at the wheel. The plea for mitigation fell on deaf ears and Faulker was fined £5 for being drunk in charge of the lorry and his licence was suspended for twelve months. To add insult to injury, he was ordered to pay £2 12s 6d in costs and was also fined 2s 6d for having no horn on the lorry.

FASHIONABLE MARRIAGE IN ARMAGH

The marriage of John Alexander Reid, late Deputy Advocate-General of Scotland, to Sara, daughter of James Lonsdale J.P., in Armagh Cathedral on 28 December 1887 was an occasion of great note and a stark illustration of the great social inequality that existed at the time. The ceremony was reported in great detail in the *Belfast News-Letter*, with a full list provided of the 'gentry of the city and surrounding neighbourhood' who were in attendance. Sara was given away by her father, James, a butter merchant and owner of the impressive Pavilion House in Armagh, who had married Harriet Rolston in 1865. The packed cathedral watched as the bride, dressed in white satin, proceeded to the altar with her father and her sisters, 'the Misses Annie, Emily, Nelly, Hetty, and Gertie Lonsdale', who wore pink satin, trimmed with moss-green velvet. The reception was held in the Pavilion before the couple departed for a tour of France. The newspapers also reported the gifts the happy couple received, noting that the bridegroom had given his bride some diamond stars, a diamond necklace, a diamond ring, together with a diamond-and-ruby brooch, a bracelet, and a gold watch. James Lonsdale gave the couple some diamond ornaments, a silver salver and household linen.

However, as with all wedding gifts, some were more welcome than others. While a Mr Gulland gave the couple a gold dessert service, the Rev. J.W. Harpur gave them merely a 'photograph in a frame'. Lady Arnott provided a lace handkerchief, Dr and Mrs Wright gave the couple a copy of *The Castles of Aberdeenshire* by William Taylor and a Mr R.F. Graham gave them a biscuit box. The presents numbered over 200 in total and ranged from the lavish to what might be described as 'tat', as was the case with Dr Leeper's silver-mounted horseshoe ink bottle. All in all, it was considered one of the most prestigious weddings that had taken place in Armagh in a long time. However, it was very likely that the happy couple would offload their oak, silver-mounted hall gong upon the arrival of their first wedding invitation.

LOUGHGALL CENTENARIAN – OR WAS HE?

Local newspapers were keen to report on the remarkable life of a William McCrea, a farmer from Loughgall, who, in July 1926, claimed to have reached the grand old age of 107. As he was talking to reporters in his kitchen in the townland of Drumherriff, William linked his good health to a lifelong pipe-smoking habit and a little drop of good whiskey. Mr McCrea had lost his sight 'several years before' and lived with his sister in the house in which he had been born in 1819. He regaled the reporters with his memories and spoke of the 'Big Wind' of 1859 and the scarcity of famine times. Despite this being a 'good news' story, William might have been somewhat economical with the truth when he claimed to have been 107 years of age. The same gentleman is listed in the Irish Census returns of 1911 as having reached the age of 79, which would make him 94 when the interviews were published in the papers. However, with such a liking for good whiskey and pipe-smoking, poor William might have aged prematurely.

THE ANGRY HUSBAND OF DERRYNOOSE

In 1810, John Lossen of Derrynoose was quite an embittered man. When his wife, Mary, left him, he saw fit to warn the readers of the *Belfast News-Letter* of the dire consequences that would befall anyone who might have the audacity to help or support his missing wife:

A Caution Regarding A Missing Wife
Whereas my wife, Mary Lossen, otherwise Montgomery, has eloped from me without any just cause or

provocation – I therefore caution the Public not to credit her anything on my account, as I will not pay any debt she may contract from the time of her elopement – And I will prosecute any Person who will, from the date hereof, harbour my said wife. Dated this 18th day of June, 1810.

JOHN X LOSSEN, Keavenhill, County Armagh

THE CURSE OF ETHER DRINKING IN ARMAGH

The practice of ether drinking across Ulster was widespread during Victorian times and persisted well into the twentieth century. The problem was particularly widespread in counties Derry, Tyrone and Armagh. In 1910, a Belfast doctor, David Calwell, did research for the *British Medical Journal* to establish the prevalence of the practice in Ulster and surveyed over 500 general practitioners to gauge the extent of ether drinking. In Armagh, thirty-two doctors responded to confirm that they had treated patients for addiction to ether. The practice is thought to have originated among the poor in Glasgow and Liverpool and then to have become fashionable in the mid-Ulster region among millworkers. The effects of the drink were said to be hallucinogenic, with a drunken state quickly being achieved and a thoroughly depressing hangover in its aftermath. In 1927, Armagh man James McCann was sentenced to three months' imprisonment for stealing items from the parochial house of Father James Fitzpatrick in Newry. When arrested and searched, it was discovered that Fitzpatrick was in a stupor and in possession of a bottle containing ether and chloroform. Despite pleading for leniency, Fitzpatrick was sent down on the recommendation of RUC District Inspector Fletcher, who told the court that 'in the interests of his [Fitzpatrick's] physical condition that he would be better off in jail for a while'.

A VERY STRANGE REQUEST FOR A HOUSE

The following appeared in the *Belfast News-Letter* on 8 November 1816:

> A young gentleman travelling last week in the county of Armagh, amused himself by reading the numerous notices affixed to a pump, in a central part of a respectable country town; among them he found the following, which he copied as a curiosity:
>
> WANTED IMMEDIATELY - To enable me to leave the House which I have for the last five years inhabited in the same plight and condition in which I found it: 500 Live Rats, for which I will GLADLY pay the sum of £5 sterling and as I cannot leave the Farm attached thereto, in the same condition in which I found it, without at least Five Millions of Dock, or Dockins [leaves], I do hereby promise a further sum of £5 sterling for said number of dockins. Signed and Dated October 1816 – NB the Rats must be fully grown, and no Cripples.

'DIRT, FLIES AND GENERAL NEGLECT' – ARMAGH ABATTOIR

'It could not be worse if you were in the wilds of Africa,' was the damning comment of Captain Noel Smith, chairman of the Armagh Health and Welfare Committee, when a report on the city abattoir was submitted by the medical officer of health, Dr. J.C. Paisley. The report was commissioned after an inspection of the abattoir by the county medical officer, following a complaint that had been received regarding meat supplied to an Armagh butcher.

Much to the embarrassment of the owners, the Ministry of Agriculture, the report stated, 'Our main abiding impressions of the abattoir are of dirt, flies, ammonia and general neglect. The premises appear to be completely unsuitable for use as an abattoir, and we recommend that it be closed as soon as possible and alternative arrangements made for the supply of meat to this area.'. The report outlined the conditions in the premises where 'there was a pool of liquid refuse a few yards outside the slaughtering chamber; two rooms were dark and completely unventilated, and smell of ammonia was so pronounced that it was impossible to remain in them for more than a few minutes'.

The members were advised that carcases were left exposed to a large swarm of bluebottles and flies and no storage room was available for storing offal, which was found hanging over a water pipe. Carcase fat was heaped on a dirty table and a yard gulley trap was blocked with blood and manure. The committee recommended that the abattoir be closed immediately and demanded that an explanation be sought from the Ministry of Agriculture.

KEADY FARMER'S DOUBTFUL INVENTION

In August 1907, Dublin newspapers were reporting that a farming man from Keady was about to patent a tyre that he claimed could not be punctured. At the time, top engineers from across the world had been battling it out to create the most reliable tyre for the burgeoning motor industry, but the aforementioned farmer proposed a novel idea which involved discarding the inner rubber tube and filling the inside of the tyre with 'tightly-packed' hay. He claimed that the new tyre would roll as smoothly as any motor car, 'without having the dread of a puncture'. Alas, history relates that the hay-filled tyre from Armagh never captured the imagination of carmakers.

8

TALES OF TRAGEDY
IN ARMAGH

TERRIBLE RAILWAY ACCIDENT
AT ARMAGH

In 1889, the annual excursion to Warrenpoint by the Abbey Street Methodist Church in Armagh took place on 12 June. What occurred 3 miles outside the city was a shocking tragedy, which was unparalleled in the history of railway accidents in Europe. In all, 88 people were killed and 263 people injured, one-third of them children. The disaster plunged the city and county into mourning and the tragic events were consigned to the collective folk memory of people in Armagh for many generations.

That morning, it had been anticipated that 800 passengers would travel on the special excursion train. However, the train was said to have had over 1,200 passengers on board as it left the station. There had been a plea by the organisers to add extra carriages, but the driver, Thomas McGrath, refused as the maximum number of thirteen had been added to the train and any further carriages, he said, would make it incapable of negotiating the steep gradients in the county.

The tragedy began to unfold when the train stalled as it tried to negotiate the summit at Dobbins Bridge. As a temporary measure to move the train over the gradient, it was decided to divide the train in two, bringing the front part to a siding in Hamiltonsbawn and then returning for the other carriages. However, after the train had been separated, the vacuum brake holding the rear carriages failed, leaving it secured merely by the handbrake and by stones which had been placed behind the rear wheels. When the driver moved the front section, it slipped back and crashed into the rear section, which became dislodged and rolled into the oncoming Belfast train. The driver of the Belfast train, Patrick Murphy, tried to slow the train, which was travelling at over 40 miles per hour, but it was too little, too late as the carriages of the runaway train disintegrated when it hit the Belfast train and its engine rolled over onto its side on the embankment. The *Freeman's Journal* described the event in all its horror:

One of the most dreadful railway disasters which have ever occurred in Ireland happened on Wednesday morning near Armagh. A Sunday school excursion train left that city for Warrenpoint with about 1,000 passengers, consisting of children and their relatives, friends and teachers. A few miles out of the city, the line rises rather sharply from the level, and here the train, which was of great length, became parted in two. The railway men said the couplings broke, others say the driver found the train too heavy for the engine and that part of it was therefore detached with the object of being brought up the incline afterwards, but no sooner had the parting taken place than the carriages forming the second half of the train began to move backward down with slow movement at first, rapidly increasing in velocity. Shouts of terror were soon raised, many people jumped out, and the train continued to speed backwards till it was running at forty miles an hour, when it crashed against the ordinary passenger train coming from Belfast. The carriages were smashed, and a vast number of persons killed and injured.

Seventy-five dead have been counted, and many of the injured are likely to die. The men in charge of the train have been arrested. So terrible was the scene at the railway that an old man who went to view it dropped dead at the sight. Many surgeons are busily employed in tending the sufferers. The city of Armagh is in mourning. There are few houses without crape on the doors.

The response to the tragedy was immense and outpourings of grief flooded Armagh city. The chairman of the town commissioners received a telegram on behalf of Queen Victoria, who was said to have been shocked by the accident. It read, 'The Queen is greatly distressed to hear of this appalling disaster, and commands me to convey her deep sympathy with the sufferers and the bereaved relatives. Her Majesty trusts the injured are doing as well as possible.' It was reported that all the coffin-makers and carpenters in Armagh were busily employed after the accident, with many coffins being sent down from Belfast. A public meeting was held in Armagh on Thursday, presided over by His Grace the Lord Primate, to provide funds for the immediate needs of the sufferers requiring pecuniary help. The Railway Company sent £200, the Duke of Abercorn £50 and 'a number of other subscriptions were announced, besides letters and resolutions of sympathy'.

There is a permanent memorial listing all those who died in the Abbey Street Methodist Church. On the 125th anniversary of the disaster in 2014, a memorial sculpture was commissioned by Armagh and Craigavon Borough Council. The sculpture, raised on a limestone plinth, was created by the artist Rory Breslin and is a life-size sculpture of a young, barefoot girl in Victorian dress, carrying a bucket and spade, as she arrived at the train station that fateful morning. Summing up the mood at the unveiling, the Mayor of Armagh, Councillor Robert Turner, said, 'The sudden removal of eighty-eight loved ones, young and old, tore the heart out of the Armagh community, then and for generations to come. The new sculpture is intended as a memorial and acknowledgement of that unforgettable day and the tragic human loss, especially the unrealised potential of the many young who died.'

POOR SERVANT GIRL ROASTED TO DEATH

In May 1901, a tragedy occurred in Armagh which ended in the death of a servant girl, Susan McGarvey, who was employed by a chemist, Mr Joshua Peel. The poor girl was in the kitchen by the fire, melting a tin of beeswax for polishing the parlour floor. While putting some turpentine into the wax, the turpentine splashed into the fire and ignited, setting fire to the unfortunate girl's apron. In a panic, she tried to discard the apron, but was unsuccessful as it was tied too tightly around her waist. Her screams of agony alerted Mr Peel and his apprentice, who rushed to the kitchen only to find her on the ground in a mass of flames which the men could not extinguish, even with the aid of a sheet. When the fire was extinguished, the girl was brought to the Armagh County Infirmary, but she died later that night from her injuries.

WHISKEY-DRINKING KILLS CHILD

On Saturday, 14 July 1860, 8-year-old Patrick Donnelly accompanied his parents to a wake house in Drumad in order to attend a funeral that morning. While there, the boy ate some unripe fruit and partook of a small glass of whiskey that was offered to him. The funeral proceeded to Armagh and a gathering took place in Armagh afterwards at which whiskey and ale were freely available. Donnelly was seen drinking heavily and, prior to leaving, was observed drinking three straight glasses of whiskey. On the way home, the boy began staggering and collapsed in the street. A cart was quickly flagged down to bring him to his home in the Mall. After being put to bed, he suffered from delirium and fits and his condition worsened during the night, prompting his family to call for Surgeon Savage, who did all he could to save the boy. Donnelly died during the night and the following day an inquest found that he had died of a brain haemorrhage brought about by a fit caused by whiskey-drinking.

THE GHOST OF THE GREEN LADY OF VICAR'S HILL

The fascinating story of the ghost of 'The Green Lady', which reputedly haunts No. 6 Vicar's Hill has fascinated the people of Armagh for decades. The Green Lady was 19-year-old Miss Bellina Prior, who was arrested in March 1888 at her mother's house on Vicar's Hill and charged with murdering a 3-year-old child, Ann Slavin, who lived with her parents on Callan Street. On a March afternoon, Bellina Prior's sister, Nina, was in the family house on Vicar Street when her sister arrived home with the young girl. Bellina then went to the kitchen with the child and half an hour later came up to her sister's room, saying, 'I have killed the child.' Nina Prior described her sister as having 'red eyes and a mad look' when she entered the room and on running to the kitchen she found the child dead in the water boiler.

The news of the murder shocked Armagh and caused a sensation when it came to court. The jury was told the full and grisly details of the murder, as well as being told that Bellina had launched an attack on her mother and brother the previous day, wielding a hatchet. The defence claimed that the child had lost her balance next to the boiler and that

Bellina had 'lost her presence of mind at not being able to save the child's life and falsely accused herself of murder'. Adele Prior, Bellina's older sister, told the court that her sister and the child had been alone for fifteen minutes when a drenched Bellina came to her 'as white as a ghost', initially saying, 'Run down, I did not do it', which Adele later claimed was actually 'I have killed the child'. Adele immediately ran to fetch her mother, Nina, who arrived at the house at 4.30 p.m. and was told by Adele, 'Mother, Bellina has killed a child.' Again, Bellina confessed and their mother ran to the library at the corner of the street to fetch Rev. Benjamin Wade.

Rev. Wade questioned Bellina in the parlour of the house and told the court that he had asked her 'What have you done?', to which she replied, 'I will give you no answer, I will not answer a word.' After further questioning, during which Prior continued to deny all knowledge of the murder, she said, 'Well I am sure I will be hanged and I will be glad of it.' It soon became evident that Prior was insane and in prison she attempted suicide by cutting her throat, whereupon she was moved to a lunatic asylum. The jury found her guilty but insane and detained her in Dundrum Asylum near Dublin at the Lord Lieutenant's pleasure.

Bellina's mother Nina moved to Dublin after the trial to be close to Bellina, who was released into the care of her mother four years' later. However, on 25 November 1909, the story took another tragic turn when police were called to 2 Charleville Road in Dublin, where they found the dead bodies of both Nina and Bellina, who had by then changed her name and was known as 'Miss Violet'. Neighbours reported to police that the blinds of the house had been drawn for three weeks and that the peace of the street had been disturbed by the barking of the family's two dogs, which were found to be in a starving condition. So distressed were the neighbours by the cries of the dogs that food was thrown to them through an open window.

The inquest was told that Bellina had been suffering from hallucinations and claimed that she had married into the wealthy Beresford family. It was reported that she affected a certain oddity of dress and was known in the neighbourhood as the 'Pink Lady' due to the fact that she almost invariably dressed in pink. Mrs Prior, who had been distressed by her daughter's condition, appears to have made detailed preparations for the tragedy and a letter was found in the house which indicated that the lady had made up her mind to kill her daughter and afterwards take her own life. The letter read, 'I leave all my possessions to my dear younger son, Harry, and I would wish him if comes across Adie [the apparently estranged sister who had been in the house on the day of the murder] to give her my fond love and some souvenir from me.' The letter continued in a tragic vein, 'I destroy my daughter that no one may get her and do away with myself immediately after.'

Evidence produced indicated that Nina had purchased two bottles of carbolic acid and that she poisoned her daughter before drinking the other bottle herself. The following verdict was returned, 'Miss Violet, or Bellina Prior, met her death at 2, Charleville Road, Rathmines, on or about the 10th of November, 1909, from carbolic acid poisoning which we believed was administered by her mother, Mrs Nina Prior, who afterwards committed suicide by partaking of the same poison during temporary insanity.'

ARMAGH *TITANIC* VICTIM'S CHILD DIES IN FIRE TRAGEDY

One of the victims of the *Titanic* disaster in April 1912 was James Heslin, who was born in Jonesborough in 1867. He married Bridget Burns, also from Jonesborough, and they settled in Liverpool, where they had four children. They returned to Armagh in 1911 and Heslin worked as a trimmer for Harland & Wolff in Belfast during the building of the *Titanic*, and was part of a team that travelled on the boat on her maiden voyage. However, James Heslin died tragically when the boat sank and his body was never recovered. Further tragedy struck the Heslin family less than a year later when their youngest child, 3-year-old James Edward Heslin, died after falling into a fire in the family's home in the townland of Edenaffa in South Armagh.

At a coroner's inquest held in Newry Workhouse, the jury was told that Bridget Heslin had left the family home on the morning of 19 March to go to fetch water, leaving her youngest daughter, Mary, and James in the kitchen. It was reported that there was a small unguarded open fire in the room and when she returned she found a neighbour, Mrs Frances Dick, in the kitchen, trying to take the clothes off the baby, who appeared to be have been badly burned. Mrs Dick explained that at about midday young Mary Heslin had come running into her house and said, 'Mrs Dick, James is all afire.' Mrs Dick ran to the house, but on her way she found the child lying by the roadside with his clothes burning fiercely around him. She carried him to a small stream nearby and extinguished the flames before carrying him back to Mrs Heslin's house, where a distressed Mrs Heslin arrived within a few moments. Both women tried to cut the smoking clothes off the child's body and it was reported that the child, despite his injuries, was able to speak and complained that he was 'very sore', but did not say how the accident had occurred. A doctor was called to the house but the child had succumbed to his injuries by the time he arrived.

Sadly, it was reported that the life of the child had not been insured, but Mrs Heslin had been awarded a considerable sum of money owing to the death of her husband on the *Titanic*. Of that money, the child was entitled to £40 and this sum was to be divided among the other children when they came of age. The child would have been 4 years old on

30 March. Witnesses told the court that they believed that all of Mrs Heslin's children had been well cared for and that the death had been a tragic accident.

SEWER GAS EXPLOSION ENDS IN TRAGEDY

On 22 July 1967, Armagh was rocked by a massive explosion which injured a number of children and killed a five-year-old boy, Brendan Donnelly. The explosion occurred on a Saturday evening at the disused Keady Railway Bridge where there had been a build-up of sewer gas and explosion close to where the children were playing. The flames shot forty feet into the air and a further explosion occurred the following evening when police and safety experts went to investigate the first blast. It is thought that the second explosion occurred when one of the men struck a match and ignited the gas, badly injuring the four men. Armagh hosted a massive funeral for young Brendan Donnelly, who lived at nearby Callan Crescent, while the four other boys, Francis McGinley, Eugene McGeown, and Timothy Vironche were detained in the Royal Victoria Hospital in Belfast.

Irish Examiner, 19 February 1894